W9-APN-548

Maryland

THE THIRTEEN COLONIES

Maryland

CRAIG A. DOHERTY

KATHERINE M. DOHERTY

Facts On File, Inc.

Maryland

Facts On File, Inc.
132 West 31st Street
New York NY 10001

Library of Congress Cataloging-in-Publication
Doherty, Craig A.
    Maryland / Craig A. Doherty and Katherine M. Doherty.
        p. cm. — (Thirteen colonies)
    Includes bibliographical references (p.) and index.
    ISBN 0-8160-5418-5
    1. Maryland—History—Colonial period, ca. 1600–1775—Juvenile literature.
    2. Maryland—History—1775–1865—Juvenile literature. I. Doherty, Katherine M.
    II. Title.
    F184.D64 2005
    975.2'02—dc22   2005000685

Text design by Erika K. Arroyo
Cover design by Semadar Megged
Maps and graph by Jeremy Eagle

Printed in the United States of America

VB FOF 10 9 8 7 6 5 4 3 2 1

This book is printed on acid-free paper.

Note on Photos

Many of the illustrations and photographs used in this book are old, historical images. The quality of the prints is not always up to current standards, as in some cases the originals are from old or poor-quality negatives or are damaged. The content of the illustrations, however, made their inclusion important despite problems in reproduction.

Contents

Introduction

In the 11th century, Vikings from Scandinavia sailed to North America. They explored the Atlantic coast and set up a few small settlements. In Newfoundland and Nova Scotia, Canada, archaeologists have found traces of these settlements. No one knows for sure why they did not establish permanent colonies. It may have been that it was too far away from their homeland. At about the same time, many Scandinavians were involved with raiding and establishing settlements along the coasts of what are now Great Britain and France. This may have offered greater rewards than traveling all the way to North America.

When the western part of the Roman Empire fell in 476, Europe lapsed into a period of almost 1,000 years of war, plague, and hardship. This period of European history is often referred to as the Dark Ages or Middle Ages. Communication between the different parts of Europe was almost nonexistent. If other Europeans knew about the Vikings' explorations westward, they left no record of it. Between the time of Viking exploration and Christopher Columbus's 1492 journey, Europe underwent many changes.

By the 15th century, Europe had experienced many advances. Trade within the area and with the Far East had created prosperity for the governments and many wealthy people. The Catholic Church had become a rich and powerful institution. Although wars would be fought and governments would come and go, the countries of Western Europe had become fairly strong. During this time, Europe rediscovered many of the arts and sciences that had

Vikings explored the Atlantic coast of North America in ships similar to this one. *(National Archives of Canada)*

existed before the fall of Rome. They also learned much from their trade with the Near and Far East. Historians refer to this time as the Renaissance, which means "rebirth."

At this time, some members of the Catholic Church did not like the direction the church was going. People such as Martin Luther and John Calvin spoke out against the church. They soon gained a number of followers who decided that they would protest and form their own churches. The members of these new churches were called Protestants. The movement to establish these new churches is called the Protestant Reformation. It would have a big impact on America as many Protestant groups would leave Europe so they could worship the way they wanted to.

In addition to religious dissent, problems arose with the overland trade routes to the Far East. The Ottoman Turks took control of the lands in the Middle East and disrupted trade. It was at this time that European explorers began trying to find a water route to the Far East. The explorers first sailed around Africa. Then an Italian named Christopher Columbus convinced the king and queen of Spain that it would be shorter to sail west to Asia rather than go around Africa. Most sailors and educated people at the time knew the world was round. However, Columbus made two errors in his calculations. First, he did not realize just how big the Earth is, and second, he did not know that the continents of North and South America blocked a westward route to Asia.

When Columbus made landfall in 1492, he believed that he was in the Indies, as the Far East was called at the time. For a period of time after Columbus, the Spanish controlled the seas and the exploration of what was called the New World. England tried to compete with the Spanish on the high seas, but their ships were no match for the floating fortresses of the Spanish Armada. These heavy ships, known as galleons, ruled the Atlantic.

In 1588, that all changed. A fleet of English ships fought a series of battles in which their smaller but faster and more maneuverable ships finally defeated the Spanish Armada. This opened up the New World to anyone willing to cross the ocean. Portugal, Holland, France, and England all funded voyages of exploration to the New World. In North America, the French explored the far north. The Spanish had already established colonies in what are now Florida, most of the Caribbean, and much of Central and South America. The Dutch

Depicted in this painting, Christopher Columbus completed three additional voyages to the Americas after his initial trip in search of a westward route to Asia in 1492. *(Library of Congress, Prints and Photographs Division [LC-USZ62-103980])*

bought Manhattan and would establish what would become New York, as well as various islands in the Caribbean and lands in South America. The English claimed most of the east coast of North America and set about creating colonies in a variety of ways.

Companies were formed in England and given royal charters to set up colonies. Some of the companies sent out military and trade expeditions to find gold and other riches. They employed men such as John Smith, Bartholomew Gosnold, and others to explore the lands they had been granted. Other companies found groups of Protestants who wanted to leave England and worked out deals that let them establish colonies. No matter what circumstances a colony was established under, the first settlers suffered hardships as

After Columbus's exploration of the Americas, the Spanish controlled the seas, largely because of their galleons, or large, heavy ships, that looked much like this model. *(Library of Congress, Prints and Photographs Division [LC-USZ62-103297])*

they tried to build communities in what to them was a wilderness. They also had to deal with the people who were already there.

Native Americans lived in every corner of the Americas. There were vast and complex civilizations in Central and South America. The city that is now known as Cahokia was located along the Mississippi River in what is today Illinois and may have had as many as 50,000 residents. The people of Cahokia built huge earthen mounds that can still be seen today. There has been a lot of speculation as to the total population of Native Americans in 1492. Some have put the number as high as 40 million people.

Most of the early explorers encountered Native Americans. They often wrote descriptions of them for the people of Europe. They also kidnapped a few of these people, took them back to Europe, and put them on display. Despite the number of Native Americans, the Europeans still claimed the land as their own. The rulers of Europe and the Catholic Church at the time felt they had a right to take any lands they wanted from people who did not share their level of technology and who were not Christians.

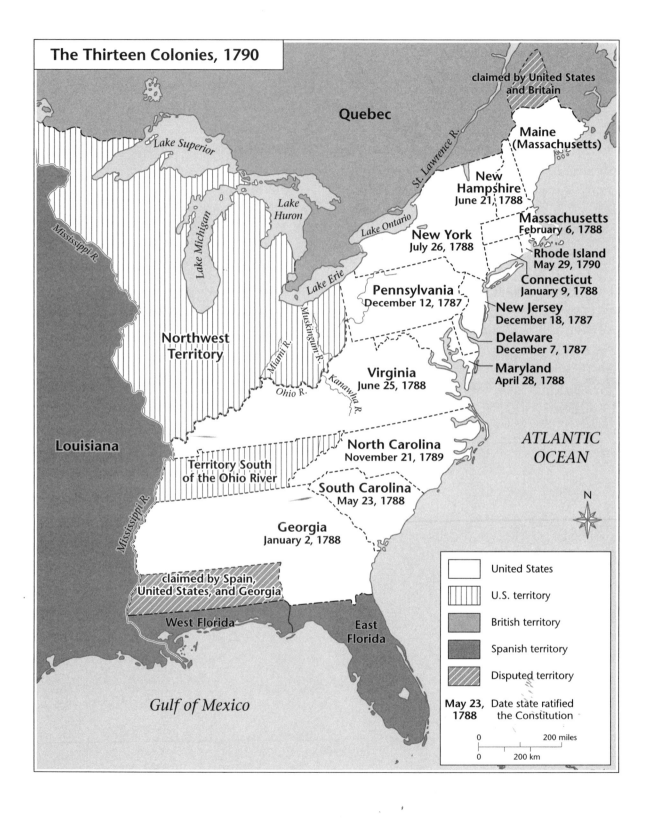

The Thirteen Colonies, 1790

claimed by United States and Britain

Quebec

Maine (Massachusetts)

Lake Superior

Lake Huron

Lake Michigan

Lake Ontario

Lake Erie

New Hampshire
June 21, 1788

Massachusetts
February 6, 1788

New York
July 26, 1788

Rhode Island
May 29, 1790

Connecticut
January 9, 1788

Pennsylvania
December 12, 1787

New Jersey
December 18, 1787

Delaware
December 7, 1787

Maryland
April 28, 1788

Mississippi R.

Northwest Territory

Muskingum R.

Miami R.

Ohio R.

Kanawha R.

Virginia
June 25, 1788

St. Lawrence R.

Louisiana

ATLANTIC OCEAN

Territory South of the Ohio River

North Carolina
November 21, 1789

South Carolina
May 23, 1788

N

Georgia
January 2, 1788

Mississippi R.

claimed by Spain, United States, and Georgia

West Florida

East Florida

Gulf of Mexico

United States

U.S. territory

British territory

Spanish territory

Disputed territory

May 23, 1788   Date state ratified the Constitution

0   200 miles
0   200 km

First Contacts

The part of North America that became the colony of Maryland was seen by a number of European explorers in the years between the voyage of Christopher Columbus in 1492 and the arrival of the first English settlers in the early 1600s. The French, Spanish, Dutch, and English all sent explorers and eventually colonists to North America. Overlapping and conflicting claims were made for much of the continent with little or no regard for the people who already inhabited the land.

Based on Columbus's voyages and the Spanish explorers and colonists who followed him, Spain laid claim to most of the Americas without even knowing the extent of what they claimed. In 1497, John Cabot sailed west for the English and explored the coast of North America from Labrador south to about latitude 38° north. This would have taken Cabot south to the vicinity of what is now the border between Virginia and Maryland on the Eastern Shore of Chesapeake Bay. Although it would be almost 100 years before the English attempted to set up a colony in what would become the thirteen colonies, they used Cabot's voyage to claim much of North America.

Giovanni da Verrazano sailed to America in 1524 in search of a passageway to China. *(National Archives of Canada)*

A French-sponsored voyage of exploration led by the Italian Giovanni da Verrazano in 1524 gave the French a claim to the east coast of North America. Verrazano may have been the first European to see Chesapeake Bay. Despite these early claims, there was little interest in establishing colonies in what would become Maryland. The Spanish had discovered the wealth of the Aztec and Inca and were growing rich off the plunder of Central and South America. For the English, most of the 16th century was a time of turmoil at home. This left little time or resources for further exploration or to attempt to colonize what had already been claimed.

The Spanish established St. Augustine, Florida, in 1565. It is the oldest continuously inhabited European community in North America. From there, they tried to establish a series of settlements up the coast in what is now Georgia, North and South Carolina, and Virginia. Some of these settlements were forts intended to help protect the Spanish treasure ships that sailed up the southern coast of North America following the favorable currents and winds of the Gulf Stream before turning east for Spain. The Spanish were also intent on converting as many of the original occupants of the Americas as possible to Catholicism and set up a number of missions to do so.

It was not until 1607 that the first permanent English colony was established in what is now Virginia. Jamestown, as the first settlement was called, struggled to survive. More than 900 of the first 1,000 colonists died of disease, starvation, or in conflicts with Native Americans. However, as time went on, Virginia began to flourish and expand. In 1608, Captain John Smith, one of the leaders in Jamestown, explored Chesapeake Bay in two separate trips. He first sailed up the Potomac River as far as what would become Washington, District of Columbia, and explored some of the other

Captain John Smith helped found Jamestown in present-day Virginia and explored Chesapeake Bay. *(National Archives of Canada)*

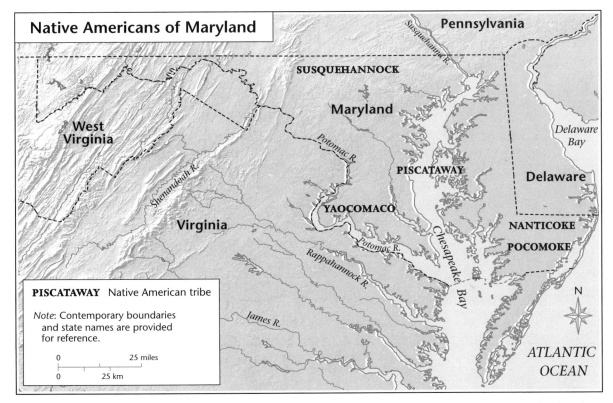

Native Americans of Maryland

Pennsylvania

SUSQUEHANNOCK

Maryland

West Virginia

Delaware Bay

Potomac R.

PISCATAWAY

Delaware

Shenandoah R.

YAOCOMACO

Virginia

Potomac R.

NANTICOKE

POCOMOKE

Rappahannock R.

PISCATAWAY Native American tribe

Note: Contemporary boundaries and state names are provided for reference.

0   25 miles

0   25 km

James R.

Chesapeake Bay

N

ATLANTIC OCEAN

The Algonquian-speaking tribes that lived around Chesapeake Bay helped the first settlers in Maryland and then moved out of the area.

rivers that flow into the middle part of the bay. On his second trip, Captain Smith sailed all the way up the bay to the point where the Susquehanna River enters. Along the way, Smith made contact with a number of Native Americans who lived on the shores of Chesapeake Bay.

THE NATIVE AMERICANS OF MARYLAND

More than 11,000 years ago, at the end of the last ice age, the first Native Americans arrived in the area that is now Maryland. These Native Americans survived by hunting and gathering wild plants. They also hunted large animals such as the wooly mammoth and the giant bison, as well as smaller animals, with stone-tipped spears. Their stone tools and the bones of the animals they ate are about the only artifacts that archaeologists have found. Between these first arrivals and the coming of the Europeans, the lifestyles of the Indians of the area evolved into a complex society based on agriculture, hunting, and fishing.

It is estimated that there were more than 500 different Native American tribes in North America when the Europeans began to arrive. The tribes spoke languages that have been broken down into approximately 50 different language families. The Native Americans of Maryland can be divided by the languages they spoke. The tribes along most of Chesapeake Bay spoke dialects or versions of Algonquian languages. The known Algonquian-speaking tribes were the Nanticoke and the Pocomoke on the eastern side of the bay, which is usually referred to as the Eastern Shore. The Yaocomaco, the Piscataway, and the Patuxent lived on the Western Shore. At the northern end of the bay and up the Susquehanna River into what is now Pennsylvania lived the Iroquoian-speaking tribe known as the Susquehannock. There was often conflict between the Algonquian- and Iroquoian-speaking groups.

There is no way to know how many Native Americans lived in what would become Maryland. However, a number of estimates have been made by modern scholars that suggest there may have been more than 15,000 people living in Maryland at the beginning of the 16th century. Although no one is sure how many people were in Maryland, the historical and archaeological record gives a fairly accurate picture of how they lived.

Despite their tribal and language differences, the Native Americans of Maryland all lived a similar lifestyle. Scientists refer to their way of living as Woodland Culture. This is because many of their needs were supplied by the extensive forests that covered eastern North America at the time. Food, clothing, and the materials to make their houses and many of their tools and utensils came from the forest. They were also accomplished farmers who grew corn, beans, and squash to eat, as well as tobacco, which they smoked during social and ceremonial occasions. It was the cultivation of tobacco that later became the main source of wealth for the some of the English colonists in Maryland.

As farmers, Native Americans excelled. They had discovered that their three main crops—corn, beans, and squash—could be grown together. Corn was planted in small hills, with several cornstalks planted in each hill. Beans were planted in the hills as well.

The bean vines would use the corn stalks for support. Beans are a legume, which means that they have the ability to add nitrogen to the soil as they grow. Corn needs lots of nitrogen, so the two plants help each other. Squash was planted in the spaces between the corn and bean hills. The large leaves of the squash plants shaded out many of the weeds, making it easier for the women of the tribe who were responsible for tending the fields.

Corn

Corn was first cultivated 7,000 years ago from a type of wild grass by Native Americans living in what is now Mexico. Over time through careful seed selection and hybridization, Native Americans were able to develop more than 700 varieties of corn.

Different varieties were needed for different purposes and growing conditions. The transition from hunting and gathering to an agriculture-based lifestyle allowed Native Americans to settle down in one area and for their populations to grow.

There are five main types of corn. Popcorn was probably the earliest type that was developed. Its small kernels open when they are heated. Flint corn is similar to popcorn but with bigger kernels and was adapted to grow in northern climates. Flour corn is a variety that can be ground into cornmeal and used to make tortillas or cornbread. Dent corn is a variety that can be both ground into meal or used whole in soups and stews. Sweet corn is the type of corn that is usually eaten fresh as corn on the cob. The Native Americans in Virginia grew all of these types of corn.

This engraving by Theodor de Bry, based on a painting by John White, records the Algonquian village of Secotan, including its crops and homes. *(Library of Congress, Prints and Photographs Division [LC-USZ62-52444])*

After a few years of use, fields would begin to lose their fertility. Then new fields would be cleared. Without modern equipment, land clearing presented a challenge for Native Americans. Over time, they had learned how to use fire in a number of ways to help them manage the land. To clear a field, they would girdle the trees (cut away the bark in a line all the way around the tree), which killed them. When the trees died, the area would be burned and then used as a new field. They also used fire in other ways. Often the woods were burned to keep down the brushy plants that grew under the forest canopy. This practice made it easier to travel in the woods and also encouraged the growth of useful plants. It also created better habitat for the native deer and turkeys that were staples in the diet of Woodland Indians.

Among the many birds and animals the Native Americans of Maryland hunted, the deer was the most important. Every part of the deer was utilized. The meat was roasted fresh as well as dried for later use. The hide was tanned and was the most important source of material for clothing and moccasins. Bones and antlers were fashioned into a variety of tools that included drills, fish hooks, scrapers, and many other useful items. The sinew, the fibrous covering on muscles, was used like string to attach stone points to spears and arrows, as bow strings, and in many other applications that might require string.

The tribes that lived along Chesapeake Bay also harvested a wide variety of fish and shellfish. The Indians fished from canoes. Each canoe was made by hollowing out and shaping a large log. They used these canoes to fish from and to travel around the bay. At the time, the bays and estuaries of what is now Maryland had many more fish and shellfish than they do today. Fish were so plentiful people were able to use a rope with a loop in it to lasso large sturgeon that ran up the rivers. They also used a variety of hooks, nets, traps, and spears to catch fish. Shells were also made into a number of useful utensils such as spoons. Shells were also fashioned into necklaces, bracelets, and headbands that many of the Indians in Maryland liked to wear.

Native American villages ranged in size from fewer than 50 people to one Susquehannock village that was reported to have several thousand residents. Often the villages were surrounded by a palisade. This was a high fence made of pointed logs. The palisade gave

Deer Hunting

Deer hunting was an important activity for the Native Americans of Maryland. Many groups considered the killing of a deer one of the indications that a boy had reached manhood. It was also an activity that was carried on in a variety of ways. The hardest way to hunt a deer was one hunter working alone. The hunter would use his knowledge of his quarry and his ability to sneak through the woods to get close enough to the deer to kill it with his bow. At other times, a group worked together to drive deer through the woods toward other hunters who were hidden.

The largest hunts might involve most of the residents of a village. They would build a large funnel-shaped fence and then would often use fire to drive the deer into the wide end of the funnel. At the narrow end, there would be a pen where waiting hunters would slaughter the deer with spears and even knives.

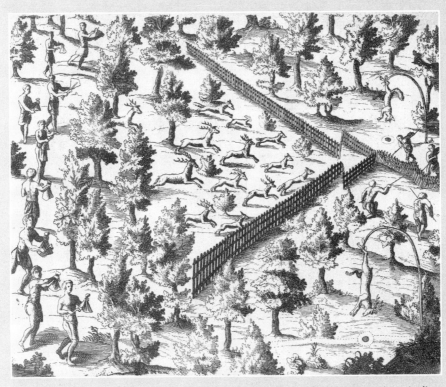

In this early 17th-century drawing by Samuel de Champlain, an American Indian deer hunt is in progress. Some American Indians startle the deer into running toward traps depicted on the right side of the image. *(National Library of Canada)*

the village protection from raids by the village's enemies. Within the palisade would be the village's houses. The Native Americans of Maryland, like others of the Woodland Culture, built two primary types of houses—wigwams and longhouses. Wigwams were circular in design. Longhouses, as their name suggests, were long and rectangular in shape.

Both styles of houses were built in a similar way. Saplings, young flexible trees, were cut down. Then their larger ends were stuck into the ground. For a wigwam, the saplings would be arranged in a circle and then bent into the center, where they were tied together to form a dome. For a longhouse, the saplings would be arranged in two parallel rows. The rows would be 12 to 25 feet apart and from 30 to more than 100 feet long. The saplings would be bent into the center to form an arch. Both types of houses were covered with bark, and a hole was left in the center for the smoke of winter cooking fires to escape. In the warm months, the cooking would be done outside.

Inside these houses were raised platforms that were used for sitting and workspace during the day and as beds at night. Longhouses were usually divided into sections that were home to one or two nuclear families of parents and their children. All the families that lived in one longhouse were usually part of one large extended family. This might include grandparents, parents, aunts and uncles, and children. The family was the most important social unit in Woodland Culture and often worked collectively to take care of the needs of the whole family. Next in importance would be the village in which the family lived. After the welfare of the family and the village was assured, people turned their attention to their tribal affiliations.

European diseases played a terrible role in the defeat of the Native Americans of Maryland and the rest of North America. Native Americans had no resistance to European diseases such as measles and mumps. However, the disease that took the greatest

The Susquehannock lived near the Susquehanna River, which flows from New York through Pennsylvania and empties into Chesapeake Bay in Maryland. This image of a Susquehannock man is a detail of a map drawn by Captain John Smith, who encountered the tribe in his travels. *(Library of Congress, Geography and Map Division)*

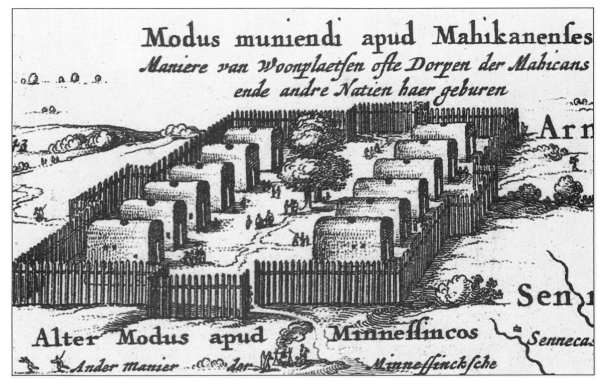

This detail of a 1685 map by Nicolaes Visscher that was based on the explorations of Henry Hudson shows longhouses, which were divided into apartments and housed multiple American Indian families. *(Library of Congress)*

toll on Native Americans was smallpox, which also affected Europeans. For Native Americans, smallpox was almost always fatal. Some scientists estimate that between 90 and 95 percent of the Native American population eventually died of European diseases. Between disease and warfare, the Native Americans of Maryland and other colonies continually lost territory to wave after wave of new arrivals from Europe.

The first Europeans to settle in what would become Maryland were often welcomed by the Algonquian-speaking tribes as they hoped the Europeans would help them in their conflicts with the Susquehannock. The earliest settlers were traders from nearby Virginia, but that all changed in 1632, when the king of England, Charles I, granted land north of the Potomac River to Cecilius Calvert, second baron Baltimore.

2

First Settlements in Maryland

George Calvert, the first Lord Baltimore, worked hard to get the rights to establish a colony near Virginia. However, he died two months before Charles I signed the charter for Maryland. It fell to his son Cecilius Calvert to act on his father's dream. *(Library of Congress, Prints and Photographs Division [LC-USZ62-102742])*

CREATING A COLONY

The original charter for the colony of Virginia was granted in 1606 and included all the land from latitude 34° to 45° north and from the Atlantic Ocean west to the Pacific Ocean. This gave Virginia all the land from approximately where the border of North and South Carolina meets the Atlantic Ocean north to the point where the border between Maine and New Brunswick meets the Atlantic. This grant included a huge portion of what is today the United States as well as some of southern Ontario, Canada. Much of the land originally granted as Virginia was later given away in other grants by James I and his descendants. Maryland, which was given to Cecilius Calvert by Charles I (James I's son), was one of many colonies that were carved out of Virginia's grant.

George Calvert, Cecilius Calvert's father, was a loyal supporter of James I who served in a number of positions in the king's government. Calvert was very interested in the expansion of England's trade and colonies and invested in the East India Company, which had exclusive rights to trade with English colonies and trading partners in Asia. Calvert was also one of the investors in the Virginia Company of London, which received a charter to establish the Jamestown colony in Virginia. In 1620, Calvert became involved in yet another overseas adventure when he bought a share of the charter for a colony in Newfoundland.

In 1621, George Calvert spent £25,000 of his own money to finance a small expedition to Newfoundland. He later received a personal grant from the king to establish his own colony in Newfoundland, which he called Avalon after the mythical land of King Arthur. In 1625, George Calvert revealed that he was a Catholic. Catholics were discriminated against in England and Calvert resigned his position in the government. At this time, in

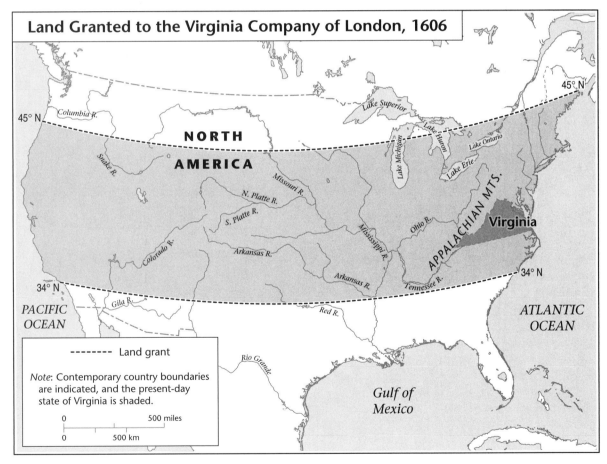

Land Granted to the Virginia Company of London, 1606

The land originally included in the Virginia grant covered a huge section of North America. However, it was quickly divided as other colonies were carved out of it.

King of Scotland from infancy, King James I inherited the English throne when Elizabeth I died in 1603 and ruled England and Ireland until his death in 1625. *(Library of Congress, Prints and Photographs Division [LC-USZ26-105812])*

appreciation for his years of service, James I gave Calvert the title of baron of Baltimore, an estate in Ireland. In the same year, James I died, and his son became King Charles I.

The newly named Lord Baltimore maintained his interests in colonial expansion and visited his Newfoundland colony twice. During his visit in summer 1629, he wrote to Charles I asking for the opportunity to start a colony somewhere else in North America where it was not so cold. After sending the letter to the king, Lord Baltimore sailed south to Virginia to visit that colony. After seeing how that colony had grown and realizing the potential for further colonization of the region, Lord Baltimore turned his attention toward starting a colony close to Virginia.

He first petitioned Charles I for land to the south of the Virginia colony. The leaders of Virginia and their agents in London did all they could to block a grant to Lord Baltimore. Eventually, the king agreed to a grant of land to the north of the Virginia colony. It has been reported that Lord Baltimore drew up the charter himself, leaving a space for the name of the colony for the king to fill in. Charles I's wife's name was Henrietta Maria, and Charles I filled in the Latin name Terra Maria, which when translated into English became Maryland. The charter for Maryland was issued by the king on June 20, 1632. Unfortunately, George Calvert, Lord Baltimore died two months before that. The charter was granted to his son Cecilius Calvert, who became the second Lord Baltimore and the proprietor of the colony of Maryland.

Charles I, king of England, Ireland, and Scotland from 1625 until his execution in 1649, named Maryland after his wife, Henrietta Maria. This painting shows Charles, Henrietta Maria, and their two sons, Charles and James. *(Library of Congress, Prints and Photographs Division [LC-D416-128])*

Many of the people in London who were involved in granting lands to the colonies in North America had never been there. They often made overlapping grants that caused problems for the colonists. In 1630, two years before the grant for Maryland was made, William Claiborne, an official in Virginia, was given permission to set up a community and trading post up Chesapeake Bay from Virginia. Claiborne and the first settlers sent to Maryland by the Calverts would literally fight over who controlled the colony.

The Land Granted to the Calverts
(June 20, 1632)

The borders of the new colony of Maryland were outlined in the charter and would be disputed throughout the colonial period by Maryland's neighboring colonies.

Know Ye therefore, that We, encouraging with our Royal Favour, the pious and noble purpose of the aforesaid Barons of Baltimore, of our special Grace, certain knowledge, and mere Motion, have Given, Granted and Confirmed, and by this our present Charter, for Us our Heirs, and Successors, do Give, Grant and Confirm, unto the aforesaid Caecilius, now Baron of Baltimore, his Heirs, and Assigns, all that Part of the Peninsula, or Chersonese, lying in the Parts of America, between the Ocean on the East and the Bay of Chesapeake on the West, divided from the Residue thereof by a Right Line drawn from the Promontory, or Head-Land, called Watkin's Point, situate upon the Bay aforesaid, near the

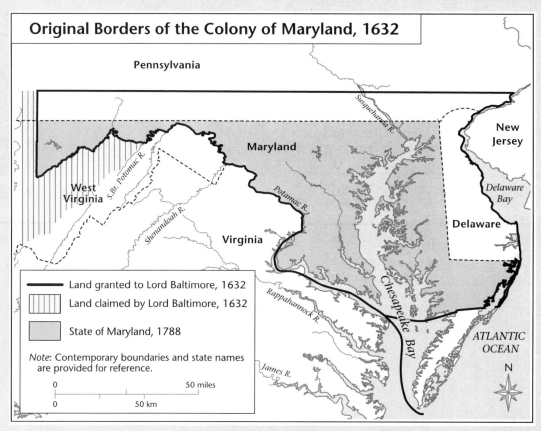

Original Borders of the Colony of Maryland, 1632

Pennsylvania

Maryland

New Jersey

West Virginia

S. Br. Potomac R.

Susquehanna R.

Potomac R.

Shenandoah R.

Virginia

Delaware Bay

Delaware

——— Land granted to Lord Baltimore, 1632

||||| Land claimed by Lord Baltimore, 1632

▓▓▓ State of Maryland, 1788

Note: Contemporary boundaries and state names are provided for reference.

Rappahannock R.

Chesapeake Bay

ATLANTIC OCEAN

N

James R.

| 0 | | 50 miles |
| 0 | | 50 km |

It would take more than 130 years before Maryland settled its border disputes with its neighboring colonies.

river Wigloo, on the West, unto the main Ocean on the East; and between that Boundary on the South, unto that Part of the Bay of Delaware on the North, which lieth under the Fortieth Degree of North Latitude from the Equinoctial, where New England is terminated; And all that Tract of Land within the Metes underwritten (that is to say) passing from the said Bay, called Delaware Bay, in a right Line, by the Degree aforesaid, unto the true meridian of the first Fountain of the River of Pattowmack, thence verging toward the South, unto the further Bank of the said River, and following the same on the West and South, unto a certain Place, called Cinquack, situate near the mouth of the said River, where it disembogues into the aforesaid Bay of Chesapeake, and thence by the shortest Line unto the aforesaid Promontory or Place, called Watkin's Point; so that the whole tract of land, divided by the Line aforesaid, between the main Ocean and Watkin's Point, unto the Promontory called Cape Charles, and every the Appendages thereof, may entirely remain excepted for ever to Us, our Heirs and Successors.

THE FIRST YEARS OF MARYLAND

In 1631, William Claiborne and a number of followers settled on an island in the middle of Chesapeake Bay, which they called Kent Island. Kent Island is just east of present-day Annapolis. It was the first European settlement in what would become Maryland. As was often the case in North America, it mattered little what was written in a charter or which country had the first claim to an area. Colonies existed and expanded based on the ability of the people there to take and hold onto the land they claimed. Often the fights were with the Indians who were there first. At other times, the parent countries of Europe fought over the rights to colonies. In the case of Maryland, the group led by William Claiborne ended up fighting the Calvert colonists.

The second baron Baltimore, Cecilius Calvert, opened an office in London after receiving the charter his father had longed for and began recruiting colonists. Leonard Calvert, George Calvert's younger son, was selected to be governor and lead the first colonists to Maryland. The charter granted Lord Baltimore complete control of the colony. The land was his to sell, give away, or rent as he saw fit. It also gave him the right to make any laws or rules he thought were needed. Because of the persecution of

Leonard Calvert led more than 150 colonists to establish the colony of Maryland in 1634. *(Library of Congress, Prints and Photographs Division [LC-USZ62-125495])*

William Claiborne established a trading post on Kent Island in 1631, three years before the colonists with Leonard Calvert landed in present-day Maryland. *(North Wind Picture Archives)*

Catholics in England, Maryland was seen as a haven where people of all faiths could practice their religion without interference from the government.

The colonies of Plymouth and Massachusetts had been set up by Puritans who wanted the freedom to practice their religion as they saw fit, but they had no tolerance for other Protestant sects and especially disliked Catholicism. Virginia followed the religious beliefs of the Crown and the protestant Anglican Church was the official church in Virginia. The tolerance promised for Maryland attracted many to the colony. About half of the first group of colonists were Catholics, while the rest belonged to a number of Protestant groups.

Lord Baltimore hired two ships, the *Ark* and the *Dove,* to take more than 150 colonists to Maryland. The Calverts used a system known as head rights to attract colonists. Any person who paid his or her own way would receive 100 acres in Maryland. Anyone who paid for the passage of five additional colonists was granted 2,000 acres. The *Ark* and the *Dove* left England on November 22, 1633.

After a difficult passage, the ships arrived at the mouth of Chesa-peake Bay on February 27, 1634. For a month they worked their way up the bay looking for a good spot to establish their colony. On March 25, 1634, the colonists went ashore on what they called St. Clements Island in the Potomac River and held a thanksgiving mass. This date is called Maryland Day and is still celebrated in Maryland today.

Governor Calvert began exploring the area for a good site for his colony. At a river the colonists called the Saint Mary's, which empties into the Potomac just before it joins the bay, Governor Calvert found a Yaocomaco village. Calvert negotiated with the tribal leaders to buy their village and land. It had been one of his father's goals that the Native Americans be treated fairly. The deal that was struck was beneficial to both sides.

The Yaocomaco were planning to move out of the area because of conflicts with the more powerful Susquehannock. The colonists received a spot that had already been cleared and a fortified village they could live in until they were able to build their own houses. The former Indian village was renamed Saint Mary's City. It

Leonard Calvert and more than 150 colonists landed in Maryland on March 25, 1634. In this 19th-century painting, Calvert and Father Andrew White, a Catholic priest, gesture to the Native Americans inhabiting the land. Visible in the background are some rowboats and the *Ark,* one of two ships they used to traverse the Atlantic Ocean. *(The Maryland Historical Society, Baltimore, Maryland)*

remained the capital of the Maryland colony for the next 60 years, when it was moved to Annapolis.

The settlers arrived in Maryland in time to plant crops almost immediately. They planted native corn as well as more familiar crops such as wheat and oats. They brought fruit trees with them and planted orchards as well. The early settlers in Saint Mary's City avoided the shortages and starvation that had plagued earlier colonies such as Jamestown in Virginia and the Plymouth Colony in what is now Massachusetts. This was because of Lord Baltimore's planning and the fact that Governor Calvert was able to negotiate for land that was already cleared.

The cooperation of the Yaocomaco helped the colonists in other ways as well. The members of the tribe who stayed with the colonists during the first year taught them many important skills that would help them survive in their new colony. The colonists

A former Yaocomaco village that Governor Leonard Calvert purchased, Saint Mary's served as a trading post and was the first capital of Maryland. *(North Wind Picture Archives)*

learned how to prepare corn in a variety of ways and were taught about native plants that could be eaten. The Indians also sold the colonists their boats and fishing gear, and then they showed them how to use it. The Yaocomaco, like many of the Indian groups in Maryland, then left the area heading west, where they hoped to escape the warfare and diseases that the Europeans had brought to North America.

The settlers in Maryland, under the direction of Governor Calvert, set about establishing the colony. They soon built a storehouse and a fort. They then began building European-style houses to live in. The earliest houses were made of wood, but those who could afford it were soon building larger brick houses on their large farms that were called manors or plantations. From the very first year, the colonists planted tobacco as a crop that could be traded for manufactured goods in England.

The Calvert family owned and controlled the colony of Maryland until they were overthrown in 1689. Built after the 1660s and photographed in 1972, this house in St. Mary's County, Maryland, belonged to William Calvert, son of Leonard Calvert. *(Library of Congress, Prints and Photographs Division [HABS, MD, 19-SCOT.V,1-3])*

EARLY CONFLICT IN MARYLAND

Almost from the beginning, Maryland was a place of conflict. In other colonies, the problems usually were between the colonists and the local Indians. However in Maryland, the conflicts were between different factions of colonists. William Claiborne and his Kent Island settlement were involved in a number of armed conflicts with the Saint Mary's City colony led by the Calverts. In addition, there was almost immediate tension between the Catholics and Protestants in the colony. This was made worse as Puritans moved from Virginia, where they were persecuted, to Maryland, which promised religious toleration. The General Assembly, which was granted to the colonists by the charter, soon found itself in conflict with Governor Calvert and his brother, the second baron Baltimore, who ruled the colony from his office in London.

As proprietor, Lord Baltimore was granted absolute control of his colony. This included the right to make and enforce any laws he wanted. The first session of the Maryland General Assembly was held in Saint Mary's City on February 26, 1635. The colonists who attended the assembly proceeded to propose and pass a number of laws for the colony. When the new laws were sent to London for Lord Baltimore to approve them, he was extremely upset. He considered the assembly's actions traitorous to the charter and himself. Lord Baltimore did not approve any of the colonists' laws. Instead, he wrote a number of laws of his own and sent them back to the colony.

Lord Baltimore expected his subjects in Maryland to respect his laws, but instead, the assembly voted down some of the new laws. This test of wills between the proprietor, Lord Baltimore, and the General Assembly would continue throughout the colonial period. Many of those who came to Maryland and the other North American colonies thought that by struggling to survive and carve new homes out of the wilderness they were entitled to have a say in their own governance. It would be this very point that would lead to the American Revolution more than 140 years later.

The conflict between Catholics and Protestants is one that is difficult for many today to understand. Almost all of the people in Maryland were from England, and both Catholics and Protestants believed in the same basic Christian doctrines. However, in the 15th century, a number of Catholics became upset with the power and corruption that existed in the Catholic Church, especially in Rome, where the head of the church, the pope, lived. The people who were upset with the church wanted reform and spoke out against the pope and the other leaders of the church. This period of time is called the Reformation, and the new churches that came into being to protest the situation in the Catholic Church were called Protestant.

Many colonists who settled in North America desired religious freedom. In this imaginary scene in a 1793 engraving, Cecilius Calvert, Lord Baltimore, shows Lycurgus, orator and founder of Sparta's government, the document establishing civil and religious liberty in Maryland in 1649. *(Library of Congress, Prints and Photographs Division [LC-USZ62-51766])*

Puritans

In England in 1532, King Henry VIII had a serious problem. He wanted to divorce his wife, Catherine of Aragon, and marry his pregnant lover, Anne Boleyn. However, the Catholic Church did not allow divorce. To solve his personal problem and strengthen the English government by taking over church property and income, Henry VIII declared the English church independent from the pope in Rome.

He was quickly granted his divorce and married Anne Boleyn, but this opened the door in England for those Protestants who also had disagreements with the Catholic Church. For many, just breaking away from the Catholic Church was not enough. They wanted more changes in the church. Those who saw little hope of the Church of England changing enough to conform to their beliefs left the church and were known as Separatists. The government in England persecuted these people, putting some in prison and forcing others to flee to Holland and other places in Europe that were more tolerant of people's differing beliefs. The Pilgrims who settled Plymouth Colony in what is now Massachusetts were Separatists seeking a place where they could worship as they saw fit.

Many other people who wanted to reform the Church of England remained members of the church. It was their belief that they would eventually be able to purify the practices of the church from within. These people were known as Puritans, and they increasingly found themselves being persecuted by the church leaders and the government. Massachusetts Bay Colony was established by Puritans. It was their intent to create a religious colony that conformed to their Puritan views. Many other Puritans left England in the first half of the 17th century and

(continues)

Henry VIII ruled England from 1509 until his death in 1547. *(Library of Congress, Prints and Photographs Division [LC-USZ62-77565])*

(continued)

moved to other colonies. Although Puritans left England to escape persecution, they thought that their way of thinking about religion was the only right way to worship. They did not tolerate other beliefs of any kind.

In England, King Henry VIII took over the Catholic Church in his country and created the Church of England.

The Puritans and other Protestants who made up the majority of the people in Maryland resented the fact that they were ruled by Catholics. In addition to the religious differences, they also disagreed with the proprietors' land policies. The people who cleared the land to create small farms believed they deserved to own their lands and did not want to pay rent to Lord Baltimore. The policies of Governor Leonard Calvert, as he was no doubt directed by his brother, Lord Baltimore, also created problems for many of the less well-to-do colonists. Wealthy people who came to the colony with indentured servants were given the first opportunities to establish their plantations. By 1642, 80 percent of the freemen in Saint Mary's City had yet to receive their own land. These people ended up leasing land or working for wages on the many large plantations that had been surveyed out along the bay.

These large plantations, called manors at the time, were intended to create a landed upper class in the colony that would mirror social conditions in England. In some ways, Maryland succeeded in creating an upper class that was based on the wealth of their tobacco plantations. However, there was also a large percentage of the population who became self-sufficient farmers on smaller pieces of land. The climate and soil of Maryland made it an almost ideal place for agriculture. In 1639, just five years after the colony was established, Maryland's planters exported more than 100,000 pounds of tobacco.

The conflicts between Protestants and Catholics, colonists and the Calverts, and wealthy planters and workers and small farmers created numerous problems in the early years of Maryland. However, the most serious threat to Maryland came from William Clai-

Located in the vicinity of Saint Mary's City, this house is believed to have been built in 1643 and is known as Cross Manor, formerly Cornwallis Manor. It is one of the first houses built by the colonists in Maryland. *(Library of Congress, Prints and Photographs Division [HABS, MD,19-SAMA.V,3-1])*

borne and his followers on Kent Island. Claiborne believed that because he had established his colony before the Calverts began colonizing Maryland, he was independent of their rule.

To prove his independence, Claiborne continued trading with the Indians in close proximity to Saint Mary's City. When Governor Calvert became aware that one of Claiborne's trading boats was working near his colony, he sent out armed colonists. They captured the men and locked them in the jail in Saint Mary's City. William Claiborne was angered by what he thought was an illegal action against his colony.

Claiborne sent the armed ship the *Cockatrice* south to seek revenge against the colonists at Saint Mary's City. Governor Calvert sent two ships from his colony, the *St. Helen* and the *St. Margaret*. The three ships came together in Pocomoke Sound on April 23, 1635, and engaged in the first naval battle fought in Chesapeake Bay. The captain of the *Cockatrice* and two of his men were killed in the first round of musket fire and the Kent Islanders were easily defeated by the two larger Maryland ships.

Governor Calvert and William Claiborne fought over the colony of Maryland in the Battle of Pocomoke Sound on April 23, 1635. *(North Wind Picture Archives)*

Although Governor Calvert's force won the battle, nothing was resolved. William Claiborne continued to cause problems along Chesapeake Bay and in London for the Maryland colony for more than 15 years after the Battle of Pocomoke Sound. In 1638, Governor Calvert sent out an armed force and took over Kent Island. This action only fanned the flames of conflict between Claiborne and the Calverts.

While all these various conflicts festered in the new colony of Maryland, people continued to come to the area. The promise of religious freedom attracted many, while others came for a chance to make money growing tobacco.

3

Life During the Early Years of Maryland

TOBACCO IN MARYLAND

Tobacco is one of many plants cultivated by American Indians that had an influence on the rest of the world. Columbus brought the first tobacco to Europe after he had seen Indians smoking it in pipes they called *tobagos*. It is from this word that the term *tobacco*

This detail of a 1752 map shows a wharf used to ship tobacco. *(Library of Congress)*

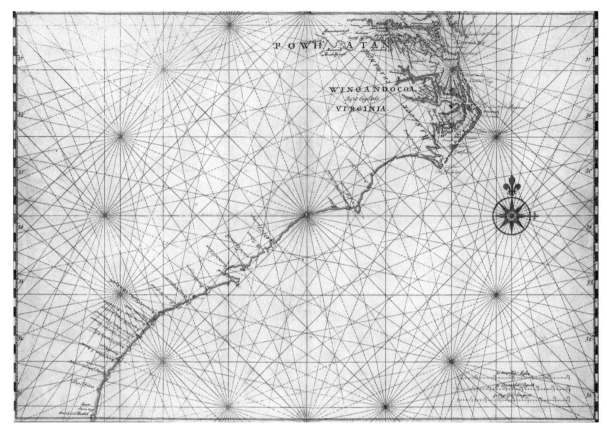

Drawn by Joan Vinckeboons in 1639, this map covers in detail the Atlantic coast from the Chesapeake Bay to Florida, including place-names and some Native American tribe names. *(Library of Congress)*

came. The idea of smoking tobacco caught on in Spain and was soon exported throughout Europe. For more than 100 years, the Spanish had a monopoly on tobacco, supplying the growing demand.

The tobacco grown by the Indians in North America was smoked in pipes during religious ceremonies. The first settlers in Virginia found the locally grown tobacco to be inferior to the tobacco the Spanish cultivated in their Caribbean colonies. In 1612, John Rolfe, a Virginia colonist, acquired some tobacco seed from the preferred Caribbean varieties and soon developed a strain of tobacco that grew well along the shores of Chesapeake Bay. Tobacco quickly became the most important part of the Virginia economy.

George Calvert saw tobacco's potential for Maryland, and his sons followed his plan. Tobacco soon became the main crop of the colony and the basis of the colony's economy. Rents, taxes, rates of pay, goods, and just about all other transactions were paid for by varying amounts of tobacco. Many Marylanders were able to create elaborate plantations based on the money they made from tobacco.

Starting a colony and growing tobacco for profit are two labor-intensive tasks. In the beginning, Maryland, like many other colonies, depended on indentured servants to do much of the work in the new colony. In 17th-century England, there was little opportunity for people to improve their lives. Many people also sought the opportunity to practice their religious beliefs without interference from the government and the official Church of England. However, many of these people could not afford to pay their passage to North America. From the very first English settlements in North America, wealthy colonists and the companies sponsoring the colonies willingly

Once a plantation home in Ridge, Maryland, this house is now inhabited by descendants of the former owner's slaves. *(Library of Congress, Prints and Photographs Division [LC-USF34-080057-D])*

Daniel Clocker came to Maryland as an indentured servant to Thomas Cornwallis, an investor in the colony. Unusually successful in this position, Clocker was ultimately able to build his own home in the vicinity of Saint Mary's City, shown here in a 1936 photograph. *(Library of Congress, Prints and Photographs Division [HABS, MD,19-SAMA.V,2-1])*

paid for people to travel to the colonies in exchange for a period of labor.

The formal agreement between the person paying for the passage to North America and a new colonist was called an indenture. People agreeing to the terms of the indenture were called indentured servants, and they agreed to work for a set period of time in exchange for their passage. Indentures lasted between four and seven years, and they often included land, food, and clothing for the indentured servants at the end of their indenture. The indentures could be sold, and often ship captains held the indentures of arriving colonists, which they would sell when they reached the colonies.

During the 17th century, nearly half of all the people who came to Maryland traveled there as indentured servants. Most of these were young men. Many who survived their period of inden-

Slavery in Maryland

When the *Ark* and *Dove* arrived at Saint Mary's City in 1634, there were people of African descent on board. One was a servant of Governor Calvert. Another was Matthias de Sousa, who may have been of mixed African and European descent. Sousa arrived in the colony as an indentured servant for Father Andrew White, one of the Catholic priests who traveled with the colonists. Records show that in 1642, Sousa attended the General Assembly as a freeman and was therefore the

Slavery was integral to the success of Maryland plantations. This small wooden building housed slaves on the Sotterly Plantation, which dates back to 1717, in the vicinity of Hollywood, Maryland. *(Library of Congress, Prints and Photographs Division [HABS, MD,19-HOLWO.V,3C-2])*

ture became successful members of the colony. Eventually, the practice of indentured servants was replaced by slaves of African descent brought into the colony from the slave markets of the Caribbean or directly from Africa.

The wealthiest people in the colony used indentured servants and slaves to create large plantations along the tidewater of Chesapeake Bay. They had large and elaborate houses built of brick. The oceangoing ships of the time could sail right up to the plantations' docks. Ships from England would come to pick up the year's tobacco crop and deliver manufactured goods from England. The manor houses of Maryland were filled with English furniture and accessories. The owners of the plantations and their families wore English clothes and ate off English china. In many ways, this small group of planters became the landed aristocracy the first baron Baltimore had envisioned.

first person of African descent to serve in a legislative body in America.

However, most of the Africans who arrived in Maryland were not as fortunate as Sousa. They were slaves who were considered the property of their owners. Special laws were passed in Maryland and other colonies protecting the property rights of slave owners, making sure that slaves were treated harshly if they tried to escape or rebel against their owners. Only the wealthiest planters in Maryland could afford to buy slaves in the 17th century.

By 1700, there were almost 30,000 people in Maryland, and just over 10 percent of the population was of African descent. Most of the people of African descent were slaves. In the 18th century, slavery became a more important part of the colony's agricultural economy, as almost one-third of the population was of African descent by the time of the American Revolution.

Slaves in Maryland, as in other southern colonies, were treated poorly. They were forced to work long hours in the fields six days a week. They were given only the most basic of food, clothing, and shelter. Unlike indentured servants, slaves had no hope of being freed after a period of service. They lived out their lives on a plantation. Although the majority of slaves were male, the children of any female slaves were also considered the property of the mother's owner. They would also live out their lives in slavery. Slavery would continue in Maryland until the Civil War in the middle of the 19th century.

MARYLAND'S FARMERS

The vast majority of colonists in Maryland neither owned slaves nor lived in elaborate manor houses. They lived on smaller farms and did most of their own work. Many had come to the colony as indentured servants and then started their own farms after completing their term of indenture. On these farms, people dressed in homespun clothes made from wool and linen, which came from flax that they harvested themselves. Often, because the majority of early settlers were male, two or more men would work together clearing the land, planting and harvesting the crops, and putting up buildings for themselves and their animals.

The houses on these farms usually started out as one-room cabins. The Swedes who had settled in nearby Delaware had introduced the log cabin to North America. Many early settlers started out with a log cabin because it was easy to build. Also, there was an abundance of trees that had to be cut down to clear the land. As these early farms grew and prospered, the owners might engage one or more indentured servants to help them. The farmers would also improve their cabins.

At first, they might add onto the cabin to create more space for their family and servants. On these farms, there was little in the

Farmers would often build a small cabin and then expand it as they were able. Built in the 1650s, this Maryland home probably began as a much smaller farmhouse. *(Library of Congress, Prints and Photographs Division [HABS, MD,19-MIL.V,2-1])*

Built in the 1670s, Resurrection Manor in Saint Mary's County, Maryland, was one of the oldest brick farmhouses in the United States before its demolition in 2002. *(Library of Congress, Prints and Photographs Division [HABS, MD, 19-HOLWO,V,1-5])*

way of imported goods. Just about everything the farmers needed was produced right on the farm. Clothing, food, furniture, soap, and other household goods were all produced by the farmers. Generally, they would only buy manufactured goods such as cooking pots and weapons, which could not be made on the farm. They would also probably buy or trade for powder and shot for their rifles. Every farmer was also a hunter and a protector who had to be ready to defend his farm against Indians or predators that might attack his livestock.

Although the first priority of these farmers was to grow enough food to survive, most of them also devoted a part of their fields to growing tobacco. Tobacco was used like cash to buy needed items and to pay taxes and rents. As a farm grew, most of the farmers in Maryland tried to replace their wooden houses with a good solid brick house. Before the development of modern building techniques and the use of efficient insulation, wooden houses were not that comfortable. It was almost impossible to keep out the drafts of cold air in the winter and the scorching heat of a Maryland summer. Brick houses were much tighter. They were easier to heat in the winter and remained cooler in the summer. Brick houses of all sizes that were built during the colonial period still stand throughout the countryside of both the Eastern and Western Shores of Chesapeake Bay in Maryland.

By 1700, Maryland was the third-largest colony, with almost 30,000 people. Only Virginia and Massachusetts, which both had more than 55,000 people, were larger. However, Maryland was still mostly a rural place. Baltimore was not established until 1729, and those towns that did exist were relatively small. Political upheaval in England starting in the middle of the 17th century caused numerous problems in the American colonies, especially in Maryland.

4

Revolution, Reform, and Restoration

Even before the colony of Maryland was established, Charles I, the king of England, was having many problems in England. In 1629, Charles dissolved the English Parliament when it refused to give him the resources that he needed to fight a war with Scotland. There were a number of Puritans in Parliament who also objected to Charles's plans for the Church of England. Many refer to this time as the Great Migration because thousands of Puritan and non-Puritan English people fled the chaos in England for the American colonies.

Charles I recalled Parliament in 1640, only to dismiss it after just three weeks. Later that year, Charles I recalled Parliament again. This Parliament would stay in session for the next 13 years during one of the darkest times in modern English history. The Puritans in Parliament and throughout the country rose up against Charles I, and a civil war began in 1642.

In Maryland, the Protestants found William Claiborne willing and able to lead their side against the royalists and Catholic supporters of Governor Calvert and Lord Baltimore. In

Charles I ruled England, Ireland, and Scotland from 1625 until his execution in 1649. *(Library of Congress, Prints and Photographs Division [LC-USZ62-91613])*

1644, Claiborne had as an ally English privateer Richard Ingle. In 1643, Ingle had been charged with treason in Maryland. In 1645, he returned to Maryland with authority from the government in London to attack any of Parliament's enemies. Ingle and Claiborne saw the Catholics of Maryland as loyal to the king and therefore opposed to the Puritan leaders of Parliament.

Ingle raised a Protestant force and in February 1645 took over Saint Mary's City. Governor Calvert fled to Virginia. Claiborne returned from England and took back his estates on Kent Island. After the capture of Saint Mary's City, Ingle sailed around Chesapeake Bay in his ship the *Reformation*, seizing the land of numerous well-to-do Catholics. After looting a plantation of its valuables, including any stored tobacco, Ingle sold the land to Protestants. Once Ingle had filled his ship with plunder and his pockets with money, he sailed back to England in April 1645.

In December 1646, Governor Leonard Calvert returned to the colony with a military force. They recaptured the capital, and the Calverts were once again in control of their colony. The governor owed his success in part to Margaret Brent, who helped him get troops together. The governor died the next spring, and Lord Baltimore appointed Thomas Green, a Catholic, to run the colony.

While Catholics and Protestants fought one another in Maryland, Puritans in England fought a civil war against the king's supporters. The Puritans were called "Roundheads" because they wore their hair in a close-cropped fashion that was in keeping with their ideas of simple dress. The king's followers wore their hair long and were referred to as *Cavaliers*, a term that had been used in the past to describe mounted knights.

Oliver Cromwell rose to the top of the Puritan army and proved to be a very capable military leader. His "New Model Army" won a number of victories and eventually defeated the forces of the king. Charles I was tried and then executed for treason on January 30, 1649. After defeating the Catholic and royalist forces in Ireland and Scotland, Oliver Cromwell became the Lord Protector of England.

The Puritan government in England wanted to make sure that Puritans in North America were in charge there as well. The colonies in New England were already run by Puritans. However, Virginia was run by a governor appointed by Charles I, and

Margaret Brent
(ca. 1600–1671)

Margaret Brent was born in England sometime around 1600. Margaret, along with her sister and two brothers, moved to Maryland in 1638. As she had paid her own passage, she demanded and eventually received 70 acres near Saint Mary's City. Margaret and her sister, Mary, lived on this land, which they called "Sister's Freehold." The sisters had also paid the passage of a number of indentured servants and were soon granted an additional 1,000 acres. Over the next few years, they continued to sponsor new colonists, and Margaret became one of the largest landowners in Maryland. She also purchased land on the Virginia side of the Potomac River.

After Richard Ingle captured Saint Mary's City in 1645 and William Claiborne had returned to the colony, Margaret helped Governor Calvert raise the troops needed to take back the capital. On his deathbed, Governor Leonard Calvert appointed Margaret Brent the attorney for his estates. This made Margaret the first female attorney in America. In her position as the attorney for the governor's estate, she was responsible for paying the colonists who had fought for the governor. Governor Calvert's estate did not have enough cash to pay all the soldiers, so Margaret went to the Maryland Council, who subsequently made her attorney-in-fact for Cecilius Calvert, Lord Baltimore. Margaret then sold some of Lord Baltimore's cattle to ensure all the soldiers were paid.

With her responsibilities as attorney for the former governor, Margaret Brent came before the Maryland General Assembly and demanded that she be given a vote in the legislature. Had she not angered Lord Baltimore by selling his cattle without his permission, she might have succeeded. However, despite the help she had provided, Governor Greene refused her request. Margaret Brent moved to her plantation in Virginia that she called "Peace" and lived there until her death in 1671.

Margaret Brent argued before the Maryland General Assembly for the right to vote in the legislature as the attorney for the deceased governor's estate. *(Maryland State Archives MSA SC 1480)*

This Dutch cartoon protests Oliver Cromwell's reign as Lord Protector of England by showing him symbolically smashing a barrel, thereby ending the so-called Long Parliament, which had been in session for 20 years. Cromwell dissolved the Parliament when he began his reign. *(Library of Congress, Prints and Photographs Division [LC-USZ62-88797])*

Oliver Cromwell was a Puritan and military leader who eventually became Lord Protector of England. *(Library of Congress, Prints and Photographs Division LC-USZ62-95711])*

Maryland was still under the control of the Catholic Lord Baltimore. To try and placate the Puritans, in 1649, Lord Baltimore replaced Greene with a Protestant named William Stone. By this time, three-quarters of the people in Maryland were Protestants. Lord Baltimore also issued the Act Concerning Religion in 1649.

This act was intended to please the Protestants in Maryland by ensuring their religious freedom. It did not work, and the civil war in England once again flared up in Maryland. On March 24 and 25, 1655, Puritan forces fought the Battle of the Severn against about 100 of Lord Baltimore's supporters. The Severn River is located near modern-day Annapolis, Maryland. During the battle, the Puritans were supported by the ship *Golden Lion*. They were able to kill or wound most of Lord Baltimore's men. A few fighters were able to escape into the woods. Those who were captured by the Puritans were hanged in the trees around the battleground.

With the Puritans in control of Maryland, the Act Concerning Religion was struck down and Catholics were forbidden from practicing their religion. For the next few years, Lord Baltimore worked to get his colony back. Finally, in 1658, Cromwell's Puritan government conceded that Lord Baltimore was the legal proprietor of the colony of Maryland. He reinstated the Act Concerning Religion, and Maryland once again became a place where all people were free to practice their own religion.

Although Cromwell's successes were in part a victory for the rising middle classes in England, the country was not really ready for the strict ideals of the Puritans. When Cromwell died in 1658, his son took over as Lord Protector. He lasted only nine months in the job before he resigned and a battle began to restore Charles II, Charles I's son, to the throne.

After a number of battles, Charles II's forces prevailed and the monarchy was restored. Charles II ruled as king of England, Scotland, and Ireland for the next 25 years. At the restoration of the monarchy, many Puritans fled to the colonies. This was a period of relative stability in England, and the king and his ministers were able to devote some of their attention to the English colonies in North America. This was good news for the Calverts, as they had been loyal supporters of Charles II's father and grandfather.

In 1661, Cecilius Calvert appointed his son, Charles Calvert, governor of Maryland. Charles Calvert ruled Maryland, first as governor and then as proprietor when his father died in 1675 and he became the third baron Baltimore, for the next 28 years. Shortly after Charles Calvert became governor, Charles II gave his brother James all the lands that were part of the Dutch colony of New Netherland. This included land in what is now New York, New Jersey, Connecticut, and Delaware. The land that would become Delaware and later the grant of Pennsylvania to William Penn created a boundary dispute for Maryland that would take many years to settle.

When Charles II died in 1685 his brother James, who had publicly announced that he was a Catholic, became king of England. Many people in England objected to having a Catholic king, and James was forced to give up his throne in 1689. He was replaced by his daughter Mary and her husband William, who was a Dutch Protestant. Under the rule of William and Mary, Charles Calvert, the third baron Baltimore lost political control of his colony. Lord Baltimore retained the rights to his lands in the colony. However, a royal governor, Sir Lionel Copley, was appointed on June 27, 1691, to run the colony.

Copley immediately abolished the religious freedom that existed in Maryland. The Church of England became the official

Charles II
(1630–1685)

Charles II was 19 years old when his father was executed in 1649. Charles, his brother James, and many of his father's supporters were forced to leave England. Scotland and parts of Ireland recognized him as king, and in 1651 he invaded England from Scotland with an army of 10,000 men. As Charles made his way south, people turned out to greet his army and proclaim him king. However, on September 3, 1651, Charles's army was defeated by Oliver Cromwell in a battle near the English town of Worcester.

Charles fled to France, where he lived in poverty until he returned as king after a royalist army defeated the Puritans. Before he could take the throne, he was forced to give more power to Parliament. Charles II ruled from 1660 until his death in 1685. During his reign, life in England was relatively calm; however, Charles was constantly in need of money to support his lavish lifestyle as king. He may have been trying to make up for the years he had lived in poverty in exile.

Charles II ruled England, Scotland, and Ireland from 1660 until his death in 1685.
(Library of Congress, Prints and Photographs Division [LC-USZ62-96910])

church of the colony. A tax of 40 pounds of tobacco a year was levied on everyone in the colony to support the church. At the same time, Maryland's 10 counties were divided into parishes, with each parish having its own official church. Catholics were not allowed to hold Mass or be baptized. By 1704, the discrimination against Catholics had expanded to the point where Catholics were not allowed to vote, and Catholic lawyers were not allowed to practice in the colony.

The second royal governor, Francis Nicholson, took over in 1694, and he moved the capital to Anne Arundel Town on the Severn River. Saint Mary's City had never flourished as the early settlers had hoped, and its location in the far southern end of the colony made it inconvenient for many of the colony's residents. Anne Arundel Town was just about at the midpoint of the bay on the Western Shore. When it became the capital, the name of the community was shortened to Annapolis. *Polis* is the Greek word for "city," which meant the name of the new capital meant "Anne city" for Princess Anne, who would later become queen of England. Annapolis remains the capital of Maryland and briefly served as the nation's capital after the American Revolution.

William III, prince of Orange, ruled England, Scotland, and Ireland jointly with Mary II from 1689 until Mary's death in 1694. Afterward, William III ruled alone until 1702. *(Library of Congress, Prints and Photographs Division [LC-USZ62-54812])*

5

Maryland in the 18th Century

The 18th century was a time of rapid growth for many of England's American colonies. Maryland, which had fewer than 30,000 people in 1700, grew to a population of more than

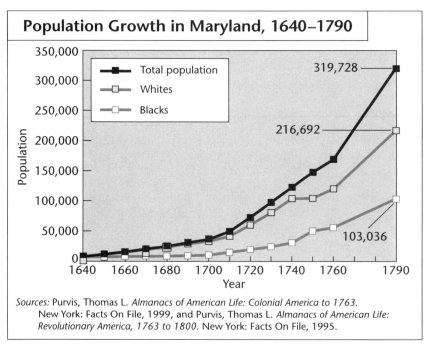

Population Growth in Maryland, 1640–1790

- Total population
- Whites
- Blacks

319,728

216,692

103,036

Population

350,000
300,000
250,000
200,000
150,000
100,000
50,000
0

1640 1660 1680 1700 1720 1740 1760 1790

Year

Sources: Purvis, Thomas L. *Almanacs of American Life: Colonial America to 1763.* New York: Facts On File, 1999, and Purvis, Thomas L. *Almanacs of American Life: Revolutionary America, 1763 to 1800.* New York: Facts On File, 1995.

Although Maryland grew slowly at first, by the time of the Revolution it had the fifth-largest population among the thirteen colonies.

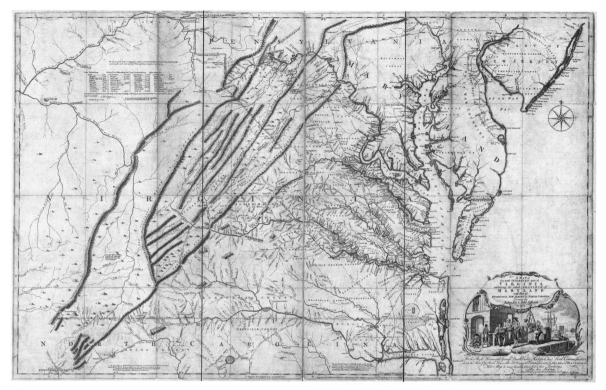

This map, drawn in 1751 by Joshua Fry and Peter Jefferson, shows the Atlantic coast, including Maryland, Pennsylvania, New Jersey, and North Carolina. *(Library of Congress)*

160,000 by 1760 and almost 320,000 by 1790. During this time, Maryland spread out from the Western Shore of Chesapeake Bay. Maryland's Eastern Shore and the lands of the colony to the north and west of the bay saw continued growth. As the population grew, there were changes in the economy of the colony as well. Iron works and shipbuilding were just two of the businesses that added to the prosperity of the colony. Many of the plantations and farms in Maryland diversified their crops as a safeguard against the unpredictable fluctuations in the price of tobacco.

THE RETURN OF THE CALVERTS

Changes were once again taking place in England. Queen Anne, the second daughter of James II, died in 1714 without a direct heir. Queen Anne was the last member of the Stuart family to sit on the throne of England. She was succeeded by her cousin George, who was the elector of Hanover in what is now Germany. He became George I, and he and his heirs would rule Great Britain until 1901. George I spent most of his time in Germany, but he was in England long enough to help the fourth baron Baltimore regain his colony.

In 1713, Benedict Leonard Calvert changed his religion. He left the Catholic Church and, with his children, joined the Church of England. When Benedict Calvert became the fourth baron Baltimore on the death of his father in 1715, George I restored the pro-

In this lithograph based on an unfinished drawing of Baltimore in 1752, the town appears quite small. Because of its large harbor and its part in the shipbuilding industry, it grew significantly during the latter half of the 18th century. *(The Maryland Historical Society, Baltimore, Maryland)*

prietorship of Maryland to him. This time the Calverts would hold onto their colony until the American Revolution gained independence for Maryland and the other 12 American colonies.

BALTIMORE

Maryland did not have a major city until after the first quarter of the 18th century. Cities such as Boston, New York, and Philadelphia in the north and Charleston, South Carolina, in the south had

become major economic and population centers. In 1729, to give Maryland its first city, the legislature voted to buy 60 acres at the mouth of the Patapsco River north of Annapolis on the Western Shore. In honor of the proprietor, they called the new town Baltimore.

Baltimore has one of the best harbors on the east coast of North America and has become an important industrial center. However, in its early years it grew slowly. By 1750, there were only 200 people in Baltimore. Baltimore became a center of shipbuilding in the colony.

There were a number of factors that contributed to Baltimore's shipbuilding industry in addition to its excellent harbor. Shipbuilders need a number of raw materials to build ships. Wood was the most important raw material, and the colony of Maryland still had an abundance of large trees that were being cut down to clear the land. In addition to wood, ships of the time needed miles of rope to support their masts and control their sails. Many of the farmers in Maryland had found it profitable to devote a portion of

Baltimore Iron Works

In 1719, the General Assembly passed a law called An Act for the Encouragement of Iron Manufacture. This law gave incentives to people who wanted to set up iron works in the colony. One of the first iron manufacturing companies was the Principio Works, which was started in 1715 by Joshua Gee near modern-day Perryville at the northern end of Chesapeake Bay. As demand for Maryland iron grew in the colonies and in Great Britain, five investors in Baltimore created the Baltimore Iron Works in 1731. The investors were Benjamin Tasker, Daniel Dulany, Charles Carroll, and the two Carroll brothers from Annapolis, Charles and Daniel.

They each put up £700 in ore-bearing land or slaves to start the company whose furnace was built on land along the Patapsco River in Baltimore. After a difficult time building the facility, the Baltimore Iron Works became one of the most successful businesses in the colony. Within two years, it was producing 14 tons of iron a week. The iron from the Baltimore Iron Works went into the ships being built in Baltimore as well as to other colonies and to England. Within 30 years, the original £700 shares were worth more than £10,000 each, and the investors made a handsome profit every year. During the American Revolution, Maryland iron was extremely important for the manufacture of rifles and other weapons. Charles Carroll of Baltimore and other members of the company were active supporters of the Revolution. Carroll served in a number of positions in the Patriot government of Maryland.

their field to the growing of hemp. The tough, long fibers of the hemp plant were the raw material that was used to make rope. Another material that was important to shipbuilding of the time was iron. Everything from nails to hold the ship together to anchors to keep the ship in harbor was made from iron. By this time in Maryland, rich deposits of iron ore had been discovered, and a number of iron works existed in the colony.

LIFE ON THE FRONTIER

By the time Baltimore was established, much of the land along Chesapeake Bay had been settled, and new arrivals in Maryland found themselves settling in the western part of the state. Most of the settlers in the 17th century, except for the African slaves imported into the colony, came from the British Isles. Settlement of western Maryland was led by people from the area of Europe that is now

Germany. The first German-speaking people arrived in Maryland in 1684, but the largest number of German-speaking immigrants came after 1732. At that time, Lord Baltimore offered any family that would settle to the west of Baltimore 200 acres of land in exchange for a modest rent. In addition, Lord Baltimore offered 100 acres to any single person who was over 15 years old. For example, if a family with teenage children came to Maryland, they would get 200 acres plus an additional 100 acres for each of their teenage children.

John Thomas Schley came with approximately 100 German families to Maryland in the 1730s. They settled approximately 50 miles northwest of Baltimore at what became Frederick, Maryland. Jonathan Hager, another German immigrant, went even farther west, where he built a cabin within the four square miles he had purchased from Lord Baltimore. The Germans who followed him to the Maryland frontier called the place Hagerstown, which it is still called today. In addition to German-speaking people from Europe, a number of Germans who had first moved to Pennsylvania moved into western Maryland.

By the middle of the 18th century, a number of land companies had been formed in Virginia with investors from London and Virginia to develop land even farther to the west. One of these companies, the First Ohio Company, wanted to develop lands in the Ohio River valley. In 1750, the company set up a trading post at what would become Cumberland, Maryland. The land speculators soon found themselves forced to deal with the French. New France stretched across what is Canada today, and the French wanted to connect their northern colony with their southern colony at New Orleans.

The French proceeded to build forts along the Mississippi River and in the Ohio River headwaters in what is now Pennsylvania but at the time was an area of conflicting claims between land speculators and colonial governments. The attempt by the French to surround the English colonies in North America was the primary cause for the fourth and final war between the French and the English colonies in North America.

THE FRENCH AND INDIAN WARS

Between 1689 and 1762, France and Great Britain went to war on four separate occasions. The first three of these wars were fought primarily in Europe, but some fighting did occur along the border between New France and the English colonies of New England and New York. The English colonists named these wars after the person who was on the English throne at the time. They were known as: King William's War (1689–97), Queen Anne's War (1702–13), and King George's War (1744–48).

Collectively, the four wars are called the French and Indian wars because the French recruited numerous Indian allies to fight against the English colonies. The fourth and final war is known as the French and Indian War (1755–62). Unlike the earlier conflicts, this war was primarily about control of North America. Most of the battles during the French and Indian War were fought in what is now western Pennsylvania, with the largest battles taking place in the area near where the Monongahela and Alleghany Rivers join to form the Ohio River. This is the site of modern-day Pittsburgh, which was first established during the war.

Many of the Indians who allied with the French had been forced out of their traditional homelands by the English colonists. Although Maryland had played little or no role in the first three wars, it was involved in the French and Indian War. After a colonial force from Virginia under the leadership of George Washington had failed to stop the French, the government in London decided it was time to take control of all of North America.

General Edward Braddock led a colonial force to march on Fort Duquesne, Pennsylvania, from Cumberland, Maryland, in 1755. The French attacked and defeated Braddock's forces before they reached the fort. *(North Wind Picture Archives)*

In the early days of 1755, General Edward Braddock arrived in America with 1,000 British troops intent on driving the French out of the area of the Ohio. Braddock and his forces knew how to fight on the open battlefields of Europe but knew nothing of the rigors of warfare in the American wilderness. Braddock enlisted

George Washington to be one of his aides and then with militia from Virginia and Maryland headed off for Fort Duquesne at the future site of Pittsburgh.

Braddock and his colonial allies met at Cumberland, Maryland, and then headed out to find Fort Duquesne. The fort was about 90 miles away, but there was no road from Cumberland into the Ohio River valley. Each day, colonial frontiersmen had to clear a way for the men, horses, and wagons of Braddock's army. They left Cumberland on June 7, 1755, and by July 9, 1755, they were getting ready to attack the French fort. The French knew that if Braddock was able to set up a siege of the fort they would not stand a chance. So, the French came out and attacked the force as it was still strung out along the road they had hacked out of the forest.

Braddock was not prepared for the French attack nor was he familiar with the style of fighting that had become common in the backwoods of America. The French and their Indian allies hid in the forest and picked off the English soldiers who were drawn up in tight formation standing out in the open. Very few French fighters

General Edward Braddock died during the French and Indian War battle he and his colonial forces fought near Fort Duquesne. *(Library of Congress, Prints and Photographs Division [LC-USZ62-50571])*

were injured in what is called the Battle of the Wilderness, but Braddock and many of his soldiers were killed, forcing them to retreat.

Although it looked like the French had the upper hand, the British finally committed enough resources to North America to drive the French out of the Ohio River valley and eventually captured all of New France. In the Treaty of Paris that was signed in 1763, all of what is now Canada and the United States between the Mississippi River and the Appalachian Mountains became part of the British Empire. Between the Battle of the Wilderness and the end of the war, there were numerous attacks along the frontier of Virginia and Maryland that were mostly small raids by Indians loyal to the French. The French and Indian War ended the major threat to the English colonies in North America. At about the same time, Maryland's border conflicts were finally resolved.

BORDER DISPUTES

The conflicting descriptions of the charters of Maryland and Pennsylvania created a serious problem for the two colonies. The original charter of Maryland extended the colony to north 40° latitude. However, when William Penn brought settlers to Pennsylvania, they established their main town, Philadelphia, south of 40° latitude. Penn in fact claimed all the land down to an east-west line that extended west from New Castle, Delaware, which was also part of Penn's grant. In addition, both Maryland and Pennsylvania claimed Delaware. As soon as people started arriving in Pennsylvania in 1682, there were problems between Penn and the Calverts. Penn returned to London in 1684 to try and settle the boundaries of his colonies. Although Pennsylvania would eventually come out ahead in the boundary dispute, it would take almost 80 years before the courts in London ruled in favor of Penn's heirs against the fifth baron Baltimore.

While the legal battle went on in England, there were numerous problems along the border between the colonies. The best-known involved Thomas Cresap. Originally, Cresap lived near what is now Harve de Grace, Maryland, where he operated a ferry across the Susquehanna River. In 1729, the Maryland legislature offered him 500 acres of land 50 miles upriver near what is now Columbia, Pennsylvania. Cresap accepted the offer and convinced a number of Marylanders to join him.

Cresap and his followers almost immediately began fighting with their Pennsylvania neighbors, who claimed the Marylanders were in the wrong colony. The problems between the two groups worsened to the point that Cresap turned his house into a crude fort. In 1734, when a group of Pennsylvanians tried to break into the Cresap house to arrest the man they called the "Maryland Monster," one of the attackers was shot and later died.

In 1736, the Pennsylvanians had had enough. An official party of 24 men attacked the Cresap house and set it on fire. As Cresap, his family, and some of his followers tried to escape, Cresap was wounded and another man was killed. The wounded Cresap was captured and taken to Philadelphia. As he was paraded down one of the main streets in Philadelphia, he is reported to have told the spectators that "... this is one of the prettiest towns in Maryland." When the Pennsylvania authorities released Cresap in 1737, he moved his family to the frontier in western Maryland. Cresap lived to be almost 100 years old and took an active role as a Maryland Patriot during the American Revolution.

In 1760, the court in England finally settled the long dispute between the Calverts and the Penns. The court divided the Eastern Shore in half between the colonies of Delaware and Maryland. The border between Pennsylvania and Maryland was set in Pennsylvania's favor, but both boundaries still needed to be surveyed.

In 1763, the two sides agreed to hire two well-known English surveyors, Charles Mason and Jeremiah Dixon, to come to America and set the boundaries based on the agreement of the two sides. Mason and Dixon established the boundaries of Delaware that are still used today. They also established the long line that now separates Pennsylvania, Maryland, and West Virginia. It took them until 1768 to finish their sur-

Charles Mason and Jeremiah Dixon established the boundary between Pennsylvania and Maryland, which later became known as the Mason-Dixon Line. This stone marker, covered by the emblems of the two states it separates, was erected between 1763 and 1767. Maryland's symbol is visible in this photograph. *(Library of Congress, Prints and Photographs Division [HABS, PA,1-ZORA.V,1-1])*

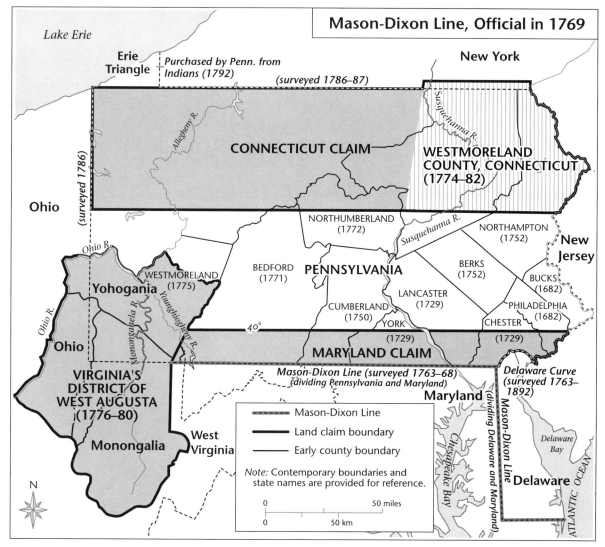

Mason-Dixon Line, Official in 1769

Lake Erie

Erie Triangle — Purchased by Penn. from Indians (1792)

New York

(surveyed 1786–87)

Ohio

(surveyed 1786)

Allegheny R.

CONNECTICUT CLAIM

Susquehanna R.

WESTMORELAND COUNTY, CONNECTICUT (1774–82)

NORTHUMBERLAND (1772)

Susquehanna R.

NORTHAMPTON (1752)

New Jersey

Ohio R.

Yohogania

WESTMORELAND (1775)

BEDFORD (1771)

PENNSYLVANIA

BERKS (1752)

BUCKS (1682)

Monongahela R.

Youghiogheny R.

CUMBERLAND (1750)

LANCASTER (1729)

PHILADELPHIA (1682)

Ohio R.

Ohio

YORK (1729)

CHESTER (1729)

VIRGINIA'S DISTRICT OF WEST AUGUSTA (1776–80)

40°

MARYLAND CLAIM

Delaware Curve (surveyed 1763–1892)

Monongalia

West Virginia

Mason-Dixon Line (surveyed 1763–68) (dividing Pennsylvania and Maryland)

Maryland

Mason-Dixon Line (dividing Delaware and Maryland)

Delaware Bay

N

——— Mason-Dixon Line
——— Land claim boundary
——— Early county boundary

Note: Contemporary boundaries and state names are provided for reference.

Chesapeake Bay

Delaware Bay

Delaware

ATLANTIC OCEAN

0   50 miles
0   50 km

After years of dispute over the colonies boundaries, the Mason-Dixon Line dividing Maryland from Delaware and Pennsylvania was finally surveyed in the late 1760s.

vey, and this line is known as the Mason-Dixon Line. In the years prior to the Civil War, this became the dividing line between the states that still allowed slavery and those that had abolished it. Today, the Mason-Dixon Line is considered the division between the northern and southern states.

With the boundaries finally set and the frontier secured from both the French and Indians, it appeared that Maryland and the other colonies would be able to go forward without any problems. However, the French and Indian War had created a massive debt for the government in London, and many in the government and in Parliament thought the colonies in North America should pay their fair share. It would be the attempts to tax the colonies over the next 12 years that would lead to the American Revolution and independence for the colonies.

6

The Road to Revolution

Over the more than 150 years that Great Britain had been developing its colonies in America and elsewhere, the government in London had passed numerous laws that were intended to regulate trade. The primary goal of the Crown was to ensure that trade in the colonies benefited the economy of Great Britain. Laws called Navigation Acts required that goods to and from the colonies be carried in English ships and come and go only to English ports. Over time, many merchants in the colonies came to ignore the various Navigation Acts because it was more profitable to conduct trade outside the tight controls of the British Empire.

Sugar and molasses from non-British colonies in the Caribbean were regularly smuggled into the ports of New England, where they were distilled into rum. The rum was then traded around the Atlantic Ocean in exchange for everything from European manufactured goods to slaves in Africa. In colonies such as Maryland and Virginia where tobacco was the main export, trade was primarily conducted within the rules set up by the various Navigation Acts. For this reason, and because many in Maryland saw the Crown as their only buffer against the power of the Calverts, Marylanders did not share the same reaction to the Sugar Act of 1764 as did the colonies in the Northeast.

THE SUGAR ACT
(April 5, 1764)

After the Treaty of Paris was signed in 1763 settling the French and Indian War, Parliament turned its attention to paying off the debt created by the war. Parliament also needed funds to maintain a large military force in its North American colonies that now included all the land east of the Mississippi River and what would become Canada. It seemed logical to the Crown and Parliament that the North American colonies pay a share of this. Many leaders in England also felt it was time to tighten control of trade in the colonies.

The first attempt to do this was called the Sugar Act. The Molasses Act of 1733 had set the tax on molasses from British colonies in the Caribbean so high that American merchants smuggled in cheaper molasses from colonies belonging to the Dutch, Spanish, and even the French during the French and Indian wars. The Sugar Act reduced the tax on sugar and molasses from British colonies but tried to make it more difficult for merchants to smuggle illegal goods into the colonies. Much of what the Sugar Act did was to help the Crown's customs service in the colonies be more effective.

Some of the merchants in New England protested these changes. However, the Sugar Act did little to change the situation for either side. The expected increase in revenue did not come about nor did the law do much to curb smuggling in the colonies. Parliament then decided it was time to create a direct tax on the people of the colonies in order to raise funds.

THE STAMP ACT
(March 22, 1765)

By 1765, the government in London had accumulated more than £120 million in debt and expected to spend £200,000 a year maintaining its forces in North America. At the time, people in England were very upset about taxes and on the average paid over 20 times the amount of taxes paid by the average person in the colonies. It was not surprising, therefore, that Parliament readily agreed to British first minister George Grenville's plan to create a stamp tax for the colonies.

The stamp tax that was proposed to Parliament required all legal documents, commercial papers, licenses, indentures, printed matter like newspapers and pamphlets, and some consumer items like playing cards and dice to have a stamp on them before they could be sold, processed, or registered. This was not a new idea. A variety of stamp taxes already existed in England and had even been used by some of the American colonies. Most of the colonies had agents in London, and they worked against the Stamp Act. However, the Stamp Act passed Parliament with almost no opposition. In the colonies, the Stamp Act set off a series of protests that probably surprised the government in England. It was the Stamp Act that set the colonies and the Crown on the path that would lead to the American Revolution.

The people of Maryland joined the other colonies in protesting the Stamp Act. When it was learned that Zachariah Hood had accepted the position of stamp agent for the colony while he was in London, the people's anger was directed at him. A dummy representing Hood was paraded through the streets of Annapolis by an angry crowd led by Samuel Chase, a lawyer who had recently been elected to the General Assembly. The crowd carried the dummy of Hood to the town's gallows, where it was hanged and then burned. Hood's arrival home from England a few days later set off another demonstration.

When affixed to goods, this stamp signified that a tax had been paid upon purchase. Many colonists felt that the British unfairly introduced these taxes when they implemented the Stamp Act in 1765, which affected goods ranging from business transactions to playing cards. *(Library of Congress, Prints and Photographs Division [LC-USZ61-539])*

This time, the crowd turned destructive as they marched to a warehouse that Hood was planning to use to store the stamps and stamped paper that he would need to carry out his new job. When they got to the small warehouse near the docks in Annapolis, the protesters set it on fire and watched as it burnt to the ground. Fearing that the angry mob would turn its attention on him, Hood went into hiding and then went off to New York, where he was safe from the wrath of Maryland's angry Patriots, as those opposed to the Crown were called.

The Sons of Liberty

When the Stamp Act was passed by Parliament in 1765, people in the colonies formed groups in their communities to protest the act. One of the few opponents of the Stamp Act in the House of Commons, Isaac Barré, called the protesters the "sons of liberty." Soon the name spread to the colonies, where it was readily adopted. It was the various Sons of Liberty groups that organized protests against the Stamp Act and later held "tea parties" in places such as Boston, New Jersey, South Carolina, and Maryland when the Tea Act of 1773 was passed.

Colonists denounce the Stamp Act in 1765. *(Library of Congress)*

Without a stamp agent, there was no one in Maryland to receive or issue the stamps, and the newspaper, courts, and certain aspects of commerce came to a halt when the Stamp Act went into effect on November 1, 1765. Although people in the colonies were upset by the Stamp Act, it was difficult for them to express why. In Maryland, Daniel Dulany, a young attorney who had just returned from studying in England, wrote a pamphlet that put the argument in terms that everyone could understand. The pamphlet was titled *Considerations on the Propriety of Imposing Taxes in the British Colonies, For the Purposes of Raising Revenue, By Act of Parliament*. Most people referred to it simply as the *Considerations*. Dulany wrote that "It is an essential principle of the English constitution that the subject will not be taxed without his consent." Throughout the colonies, Dulaney's argument was simplified to "No taxation without representation."

The *Considerations* were widely circulated in Maryland, and editions of it were printed and distributed in Boston and New York. There were even copies of the pamphlet published in London, where opponents to the Stamp Act adopted Delaney's arguments to fight for repeal of the law. Throughout winter 1765–66, the

A lawyer who actively protested the Stamp Act, Samuel Chase represented Maryland at the First and Second Continental Congresses and signed the Declaration of Independence on behalf of the colony. *(Library of Congress, Prints and Photographs Division [LC-USZ62-65448])*

Stamp Act Congress
(October 1765)

As the date for the Stamp Act to go into effect (November 1, 1765) neared, the Massachusetts assembly sent a letter to all the other colonies asking then to send delegates to New York to discuss what could be done about the Stamp Act. Nine colonies, including Maryland, sent delegates to New York in October 1765. There was little talk of independence at the congress. The colonial leaders were still loyal to the king and saw Parliament as their enemy. The delegates wanted to make their position clear to the king, who they hoped would step in on their behalf with Parliament. The congress sent the king a petition that included 14 resolutions. Two of the most important were:

"That His Majesty's liege subjects in these colonies, are entitled to all the inherent rights and liberties of his natural born subjects within the kingdom of Great-Britain.

That it is inseparably essential to the freedom of a people, and the undoubted right of Englishmen, that no taxes be imposed on them, but with their own consent, given personally, or by their representatives."

The beginning of the Stamp Act appears as printed in a 1766 manuscript in London. Its 1765 passage sparked protests by the colonists. *(Library of Congress)*

courts in Maryland remained closed, and a number of other businesses found it hard to do their work without the required stamps. Toward the end of January 1766, word came to Maryland that courts in other colonies had reopened and were conducting business without stamped paper. The court in Frederick County was the first to return to business.

On January 30, 1766, the *Maryland Gazette* reopened in defiance of the Stamp Act and called upon other courts and businesses to do the same. In February, the Sons of Liberty from Baltimore and Anne Arundel counties confronted the colonial government in Annapolis in an attempt to get them to officially come out against the Stamp Act. Not everyone in Maryland agreed with the actions of the Sons of Liberty, but the problems of the Stamp Act disappeared when word arrived in the colony that the Stamp Act had been repealed by Parliament on March 18, 1766. It looked like the first round between the Crown and the colonies had been won by the colonies. When Parliament repealed the Stamp Act, they passed the Declaratory Act. This law stated that Parliament believed it had the right to pass any laws that it thought were needed to govern any and all British colonies.

THE TOWNSHEND DUTIES
(June 29, 1767)

A little more than a year after the repeal of the Stamp Act, Parliament came up with another plan to raise revenue from the American colonies. One of the objections made about the Stamp tax was that it was a direct tax on people who had no voice in Parliament. This time Charles Townshend, a leader in Parliament, suggested a series of indirect taxes on goods the colonies needed to import from England. This made sense to many in Parliament, especially since the Pennsylvania agent, Benjamin Franklin, had argued this very distinction before Parliament during the arguments over the Stamp Act.

On July 29, 1767, Parliament passed the duties proposed by Townshend and placed taxes on glass, lead, painter's colors, paper, and tea that were to be paid by the importers and not directly by the residents of the colony. The buyers of these goods would indirectly pay the taxes as prices on these goods were raised to cover the cost of the tax. At first, many in the colonies did not know how to react to the Townshend Duties and protests were slow in developing.

Patriots in the Massachusetts legislature, which was one of the hotbeds of feelings against the Crown, issued what is known as the Massachusetts Circular Letter in February 1767. The letter agreed that Parliament had the right to pass laws for the British Empire as a whole but did not have the right to tax the colonies either directly or indirectly without the consent of the people being taxed. Over time, merchants throughout the colonies agreed not to

Liberty Tree

Throughout the colonies, the Sons of Liberty designated meeting places. These were often outdoors under the spreading limbs of a tree. These trees became known as Liberty Trees. The one in Boston, Massachusetts, was a giant elm that was cut down by British soldiers during the Siege of Boston in 1775. It supposedly yielded 14 cords of firewood. The Liberty Tree in Charleston, South Carolina, was an oak. When the city was captured by the British in 1780, they cut down the tree and then burned the stump. The Patriots of Charleston dug up the roots of the Liberty Tree and made canes out of them. Reportedly, Thomas Jefferson was presented with a cane from the roots of the Charleston Liberty Tree. The last remaining Liberty Tree from the time of the American Revolution was a huge poplar on the campus of St. John's College in Annapolis, Maryland. Over the years, people went to great lengths to keep the tree alive. It was finally cut down in 1999 after it was severely damaged by a hurricane.

The last remaining Liberty Tree, shown on the campus of St. John's College in Annapolis, Maryland, in a 1906 photograph, stood until 1999. *(Library of Congress, Prints and Photographs Division [LC-D4-19117])*

Paul Revere's engraving of the Boston Massacre depicts the event that many consider the beginning of the struggle for independence. It occurred on March 5, 1770. *(Library of Congress, Prints and Photographs Division [LC-USZ62-35522])*

import goods that were included in the Townshend Duties. On March 20, 1769, many of the merchants in Baltimore reluctantly followed the lead of merchants in Philadelphia and other major ports by forming what was called a nonimportation association.

Protests over the Townshend Duties turned violent during winter 1770. In New York City, on January 18, 1770, British soldiers who had been taking work away from New York laborers while on leave clashed in what is known as the Battle of Golden Hill. In the fight, numerous people on both sides were injured, but there were no fatalities. The same was not true on March 5, 1770, when a large mob of Patriot protesters assembled outside the customshouse in Boston. The crowd verbally abused and threw ice and snowballs at the soldiers guarding the customshouse. The soldiers reportedly raised their muskets and aimed them at the crowd. It was never discovered who gave the order, but someone yelled "fire!" and the soldiers shot into the mob. Five people died and six others were wounded in what is known as the Boston Massacre.

In April 1770, Parliament repealed all the Townshend Duties except the one on tea. The duty on tea was kept only as a symbol of Parliament's authority. Repeal of the Townshend Duties brought about a period of relative calm in the colonies. Had Parliament stopped there, the 13 American colonies might still be a part of the British Commonwealth. However, problems with the trade from Asia caused Parliament to once again stir up Patriot sentiment in the colonies.

THE TEA ACT
(May 10, 1773)

The British East India Company had been set up to conduct all the trade between England and its colonies and trading partners in Asia. Tea was the company's most important trade item. Under the rules at the time, the company had to bring all its tea to England and sell it to wholesalers who then increased the price and reshipped it all over the empire, including to the American colonies. When the tea arrived in the American colonies, it was sold to another layer of wholesalers, who again marked up the price of the tea. This made English tea very expensive, and many people drank tea that was smuggled in by Dutch traders. The smuggled Dutch tea was much cheaper than the "legal" English tea.

By 1773, the British East India Company was on the verge of bankruptcy. Many people in the government owned stock in the company and wanted to protect their investment. On May 10, 1773, Parliament passed a law known as the Tea Act. This law allowed the company to sell tea directly to the American colonies, skipping the wholesalers in both England and America. The law also gave the company a monopoly on tea sales. People in England assumed that the colonists would welcome the Tea Act, as it would actually reduce the price they paid for English tea.

However, by this time the Patriots in the colonies were looking for reasons to defy the Crown, and the Tea Act gave them the perfect opportunity. Groups led by the Sons of Liberty called for a boycott of English tea and people began drinking a variety of brews made from local plants that they called "liberty tea."

When the first shipment of "cheaper" tea arrived in Boston on December 16, 1773, a group of about 60 men, most of whom were members of the Sons of Liberty, disguised as Indians, snuck

To protest the passage of the Tea Act, some male colonists, disguised as American Indians, boarded three ships in Boston Harbor on December 16, 1773, and dumped hundreds of cases of tea into the harbor. The event became known as the Boston Tea Party. *(Library of Congress, Prints and Photographs Division [LC-USZ61-450])*

onto the tea ships and dumped about £10,000 worth of tea into Boston Harbor.

The event was soon known as the Boston Tea Party, and it was copied in a number of other communities throughout the colonies. In Maryland, English tea arrived on the ship *Peggy Stewart*, which was owned by Anthony Stewart of Annapolis. When the *Peggy Stewart* arrived in Annapolis on October 15, 1774, the people of Annapolis, led by the Sons of Liberty, turned their anger toward Stewart. There was a public debate whether the crowd should burn Stewart's house or hang him if he tried to bring his tea ashore. Rather than suffer the anger of the mob, Stewart went out into the

Owned at various times by Thomas Stone and Daniel of St. Thomas Jenifer, this house in Annapolis, Maryland, is known as the Peggy Stewart House. Anthony Stewart, the merchant who owned the *Peggy Stewart* ship, owned the house in the 1770s. Both the ship and the house are named for Stewart's daughter. *(Library of Congress, Prints and Photographs Division [HABS, MD,2-ANNA,15-1])*

harbor on October 19, 1774, and set his own ship on fire. As the flames of the *Peggy Stewart* were drowned out in the harbor of Annapolis, many Patriots were fanning the flames of conflict with the Crown at the First Continental Congress in Philadelphia as the colonies reacted to the Intolerable Acts.

THE INTOLERABLE ACTS
(1774)

After the Boston Tea Party, Parliament and the Crown had had enough. George III and his first minister, Lord North, decided it was time to teach the upstart colonials of Boston a lesson. Parliament proceeded to enact five new laws that were called the Coercive Acts in England. In the colonies, they were simply called the Intolerable Acts. The first of these acts, known as the Boston Port Bill (March 31, 1774), closed Boston Harbor until the city paid £10,000 for the destroyed tea. The second law was called the Massachusetts Government Act (May 20, 1774) and made major changes to the charter of the colony to force tighter Crown control on the people of Massachusetts. The other three acts dealt with taking authority away from local courts in the colonies, the quartering of British troops in the colonies, and giving special privileges to Canada, which had not participated in any of the protests.

People throughout the colonies were outraged and frightened by this show of force by the Crown. They reasoned that if it could happen in Boston and Massachusetts, it could happen to them as well. Many in Maryland sent food and other needed goods to Boston by various routes to avoid the blockade of the harbor.

THE FIRST CONTINENTAL CONGRESS
(1774)

After the passage of the Intolerable Acts, Patriot leaders in the colonies called for a meeting of representatives from all the colonies to address the problems between the colonies and the Crown. The meeting was set for September 5, 1774, in Philadelphia and is called the First Continental Congress. All of the colonies except Georgia sent delegates to the congress. Maryland sent Samuel Chase, Robert Goldsborough, Thomas Johnson, William Paca, and Mathew Tilghman. Although some of the more radical

The First Continental Congress met in Philadelphia and composed and sent resolutions to the king of Great Britain. They planned a second congress for the following spring to assess their situation. *(Library of Congress, Prints and Photographs Division [LC-USZ62-45328])*

Patriots at the congress were talking about independence, the majority of delegates were still interested in working out their differences with the Crown.

After almost two months of debate, a series of resolutions were drafted and sent to the king. The delegates also agreed to support a series of nonviolent actions that primarily involved embargoes against trading with Great Britain.

The delegates agreed to return the following year to evaluate the progress they had made in solving their problems with Lon-

The Resolutions of
the First Continental Congress

After listing numerous complaints with the attempts by Parliament to impose its will on the American colonies, the document sent to the king by the First Continental Congress made it clear that the Americans were planning boycott, not revolution.

"Resolved, unanimously, That from and after the first day of December next, there be no importation into British America, from Great Britain or Ireland of any goods, wares or merchandize whatsoever, or from any other place of any such goods, wares or merchandize."

don. They also realized that the Crown might not give in this time, and the congress suggested the colonies start drilling their militias in case the British forces stationed in the colonies were instructed to take action.

7

Fighting for Independence

While the colonies agreed to work together at the First Continental Congress in Philadelphia, the Patriot leaders in Maryland took their own steps to gain control of the colonial government. In part in reaction to the closing of the port of Boston, the Committee of Correspondence in Annapolis suggested that it was time to break away from the proprietary government that had ruled Maryland, with only a couple of interruptions, since the *Dove* and *Ark* had arrived in 1634. The Patriot leaders suggested that the counties in Maryland needed to send representatives to a colony-wide meeting to discuss the problems with the Crown.

On June 24, 1774, 92 representatives met in what was called the provincial congress. This marked the end of the proprietary government in Maryland, as the General Assembly would not meet again until after Maryland was part of the United States. Many still hoped to avoid war, but Maryland planned to be ready if it came. Militia groups around Maryland began drilling. Others in Maryland, like the Baltimore Iron Works, began making war materials to support the Patriot cause. The provincial convention selected delegates to go to the Second Continental Congress in May 1775. Many still hoped that war could be avoided, but on April 28, 1775, a message arrived in Baltimore that fighting had broken out between British soldiers and Patriots in Massachusetts.

THE BATTLES OF LEXINGTON AND CONCORD
(April 19, 1775)

Early on the morning of April 19, 1775, approximately 800 hand-picked British soldiers arrived on the town common in Lexington, Massachusetts. They had come to arrest some of the Patriot leaders who were reported to be in the area and to seize a supply of weapons that was supposedly hidden at a farm in nearby Concord. Instead, they found 70 minutemen waiting for them. The minutemen, as the Massachusetts militia was called, had been warned by Paul Revere and other riders from Boston that the British were on the move. When the British officer in charge ordered the colonials to surrender, they tried to run away. No one knows who fired first, but British soldiers got off two volleys before they stopped shooting. When the smoke from their muskets cleared the common, eight colonials were found dead and another 10 were wounded.

When the British reached the North Bridge in Concord, they were met by a much more substantial Patriot force and had to retreat

The Battles of Lexington (shown here) and Concord signaled the beginning of the Revolutionary War. *(National Archives/DOD, War & Conflict, #10)*

all the way to Boston. Along the way, colonial sharpshooters killed or wounded 273 of the "redcoats," which is what the Patriots called the British soldiers because they wore bright red uniforms. When the delegates to the Second Continental Congress arrived in Philadelphia a few weeks later, the entire situation had changed.

THE SECOND CONTINENTAL CONGRESS (1775–1789)

The Second Continental Congress convened on May 10, 1775, and remained the governing body of the Patriots and then the united colonies until the U.S. Constitution was enacted in 1789. Fifty of the 65 delegates had also attended the First Continental Congress. Many in the congress wanted to talk about independence. However, before the congress could address the issue of independence, they had to deal with the more immediate problems of the siege of Boston. Some delegates still hoped to reconcile with the Crown, and they wrote the "Olive Branch Petition," which was sent to the king in hopes that he would repeal the Intolerable Acts and stop any further fighting in Boston.

After the Battles of Lexington and Concord, thousands of colonial militia had surrounded Boston and the British forces that held it. On June 17, 1775, the Battle of Bunker Hill made it clear that reconciliation was out of the question. At Bunker Hill in Charlestown, Massachusetts, colonial forces fought a major battle with the British army. Although the British ultimately drove the Patriot forces from Breed's Hill and Bunker Hill, 226 soldiers were killed and 828 wounded, while the colonials suffered 140 killed and 271 wounded. The British commanders had only a limited number of soldiers available in North America and could not afford to "win" battles where they sustained that many casualties.

In Philadelphia, one of the first official acts of the Congress was to create a continental army and appoint George Washington as commanding general. Washington and many of the soldiers who fought with him brought their experiences in the French and Indian War to bear on their struggle against the British. Washington's first task was to take command of the siege of Boston. He went north with soldiers from Maryland, Virginia, and Pennsylvania. Soldiers from Maryland would be with Washington throughout the war and would play an important role in a number of major battles. By the following spring, 1776, using cannons that had been transported over the snow from Fort Ticonderoga on Lake Champlain, Washington was victorious. The British evacuated Boston on March 17, 1776.

Even though most believed that further conflict was likely, many delegates were still not ready to vote for independence. One

The Second Continental Congress convened on May 10, 1775, and remained in session until the newly independent nation had a constitution. *(National Archives, Still Picture Records, NWDNS-148-CCD-35)*

of the events that pushed many in the colonies toward declaring independence was the publishing of Thomas Paine's pamphlet *Common Sense*. Paine wrote about the reasons why the colonies should become independent from Britain. Prior to the publication of Paine's pamphlet *Common Sense*, the arguments had not been presented in terms that the average person could understand. Paine's pamphlet was an immediate success. It was published on January 10, 1776, and sold 100,000 copies in the first three months; 500,000 copies would eventually be distributed. Considering that there were only 2.5 million people in the American colonies, that is an amazing number.

While *Common Sense* swayed public opinion in favor of independence and George Washington succeeded in Boston, fellow Virginian Thomas Jefferson took the lead in Philadelphia. With help from Benjamin Franklin of Pennsylvania and John Adams from Massachusetts, Jefferson wrote the document that would change the course of history.

A Revolutionary War leader, Thomas Paine wrote the popular pamphlet *Common Sense*. *(National Archives/ DOD, War & Conflict, #63)*

In the process of approving the Declaration of Independence, the congress had agreed that each colony, no matter how many delegates they sent or how many people they represented, would have one vote. When the state delegations to the Second Continental Congress were polled on July 1, 1776, it looked like only nine states, including Maryland, were ready to vote in favor of the Declaration of Independence. Only two delegates from Delaware were present, and one voted for and one against. The delegates from New York had been instructed not to vote until the Patriot legislature sent them instructions. The delegates from Pennsylvania and South Carolina voted against the declaration.

The Pennsylvania delegation consisted of seven members. In the first round, they voted four to three against independence. On

July 2, when the delegations were again polled, John Dickinson and Robert Morris did not vote, and the rest of the Pennsylvania delegation voted three to two in favor of independence. The South Carolina delegates said they would not stand alone and would vote with the 11 colonies that had already agreed to independence. The New York delegates still did not vote, but they assured the Congress that they would vote in the affirmative as soon as they got the official go-ahead from home.

On July 2, 1776, the delegates voted 12 to zero in favor of independence. Two days later on July 4, 1776, the Declaration of Independence passed by the same vote, and the idea of reconciling with Parliament and the Crown was set aside. On July 9, 1776, New York made the vote unanimous. Then on August 2, 1776, a ceremony was held for the delegates to sign the Declaration of Independence. As president of the Congress, John Hancock of Massachusetts was the first of 56 delegates to sign.

Copies of the Declaration of Independence were circulated and read throughout the colonies. Many

Charles Carroll of Carrollton signed the Declaration of Independence on behalf of Maryland. *(Library of Congress, Prints and Photographs Division [LC-USZ62-64714])*

One of the first and boldest acts of the Second Continental Congress was to compose and sign the Declaration of Independence in summer 1776. *(Library of Congress)*

people rallied to the cause of independence. However, it took more than a declaration to make the colonies independent. It took a long and costly war before they became the United States.

Thomas Stone represented Maryland at the Second Continental Congress, during which he signed the Declaration of Independence on behalf of the colony.
(Library of Congress, Prints and Photographs Division [LC-USZ61-203])

MARYLANDERS IN THE AMERICAN REVOLUTION

Soldiers from Maryland went north to the Siege of Boston with George Washington, whose plantation Mount Vernon was just across the Potomac River from Maryland. When Washington moved his forces to New York to keep the British from taking the city, the Maryland troops stayed with him. Trying to defend New York was more than the new Continental army could do. The British sent a large force of seasoned troops to take on Washington's ragtag army.

The first part of the struggle to hang onto New York is known as the Battle of Long Island. Washington had fortified a line on the western end of Long Island in hopes of blocking the British entry to Manhattan. The British commander, General Howe, spent four days doing reconnaissance on Washington's position. On August 27, 10,000 Americans faced 20,000 regular British and mercenary soldiers, known as Hessians, as Howe attacked Washington's unprotected eastern flank. The British worked to surround Washington's army and forced them back to the fortified Brooklyn Heights.

More than 2,000 Americans were killed, wounded, or captured. The British losses were only 400 men. Had Howe pushed his advantage on Brooklyn Heights, the Revolution might have ended in that one battle. However, Howe decided to prepare to bombard the Heights. Realizing the futility of his position, Washington took advantage of a foggy summer night to slip back across the East River with all his troops and equipment. As Washington snuck away, troops from Maryland were given the job of covering the retreat.

Washington was so impressed with the courage of his Maryland troops that he is reported to have later said, "No troops poured out their blood more freely for the common cause than

Under the command of General William Howe, the British defeated the colonial forces during the Battle of Long Island. Troops from Maryland covered the forces as General George Washington led the retreat. *(National Archives/DOD War & Conflict, #28)*

those of Maryland." For their actions as the rearguard at the Battle of Long Island, the Maryland troops were nicknamed the "Old Line." It is a name they took pride in, and it was later adopted as the nickname for the state of Maryland, which is still known as "The Old Line State."

After the Battle of Long Island, the Continental army retreated across New Jersey and into Pennsylvania. For the next two years, Washington and the British played a game of cat and mouse in

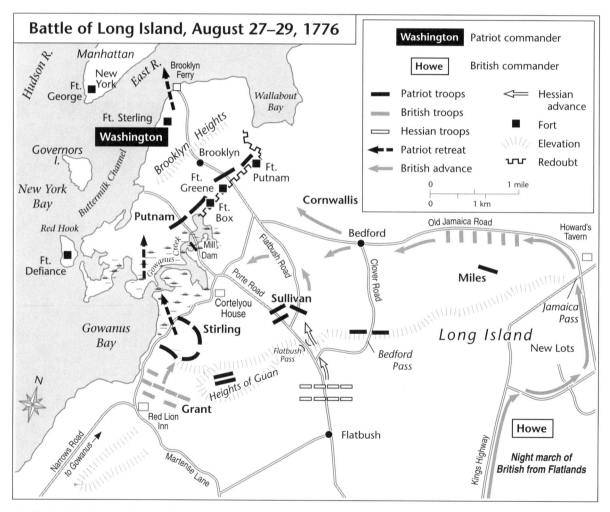

Battle of Long Island, August 27–29, 1776

At the Battle of Long Island, New York, troops from Maryland served as the rear guard, allowing the Continental army to retreat successfully to Manhattan. This duty earned them the nickname the "Old Line" from General George Washington.

The British forces defeated the colonists at the Battle of Brandywine on September 11, 1777. *(Library of Congress, Prints and Photographs Division [LC-USZ62-100726])*

New Jersey. Finally the British changed their tactics and headed south from New York by ship. The British General Howe left New York on 260 ships with 18,000 men under his command. Everyone assumed they were headed for Philadelphia, but no one was sure how they would get there.

Soon the British fleet appeared in Chesapeake Bay. They sailed up the Bay to the Elk River in Maryland. There they landed their forces and headed to Philadelphia. The Patriot forces were soundly defeated at the Battle of Brandywine in Pennsylvania and were forced to spend the very cold and snowy winter of 1777–78 in Valley Forge, Pennsylvania. That winter marked a major change in the Continental army.

After suffering through the winter, the situation slowly improved. As spring approached, food began to arrive more regularly as did other supplies. Baron Frederich Wilhelm von Steuben joined Washington at Valley Forge at the end of February 1778 and had a positive affect on the entire army.

Baron Frederich Wilhelm von Steuben
(1730–1794)

While in Paris in 1777, Benjamin Franklin was introduced to a Prussian army officer who had fought in a number of European wars and had been on Frederick the Great's general staff. Baron Frederich Wilhelm von Steuben was living in Paris on his half-pay pension as a captain. Franklin convinced Steuben to go to America and offer his services to the Continental Congress. Steuben told the congress that he was a lieutenant general, and he was appointed acting inspector general of the Continental army by George Washington. Steuben is credited with reorganizing Washington's army and teaching the troops at Valley Forge the discipline that made European armies more efficient fighting forces. In addition to drilling the soldiers at Valley Forge, Steuben wrote the army's first manual of procedures.

Baron Frederich Wilhelm von Steuben reorganized and strengthened the Continental army. *(National Archives/DOD, War & Conflict, #59)*

Steuben fashioned Washington's army into a much more disciplined and effective fighting force. The soldiers gained confidence from his instruction. The force that marched out of Valley Forge on June 19, 1778, was much more ready to fight the British than the one that had been defeated at Brandywine.

Steuben was not the only European to come to the aid of the American cause. Other well-known European soldiers arrived to fight with Washington. The marquis de Lafayette, the young French nobleman who would become an aide and confidante of General Washington, first arrived in Baltimore in 1777. Lafayette purchased ammunition, clothing, and food to give to the Patriots. He also recruited a number of Marylanders to join him when he went north to join up with Washington.

Although there were no battles fought in Maryland, Chesapeake Bay was the home to numerous privateers who attacked British merchant ships throughout the war. At the time of the American Revolution, the British had the largest navy in the world. When the Continental Congress declared independence in 1776, they were quick to form the Continental army, but creating a navy was a much greater challenge. Ships had to be built and outfitted before there could be a navy. Although Rhode Island assisted in starting a navy, it was never a real factor in the war.

Privateers were a much more efficient way for the colonies to disrupt British supplies. A privateer was the name given to ships

General George Washington and his troops spent the winter of 1777 to 1778 at Valley Forge, Pennsylvania, about 20 miles from Philadelphia, occupied, at that time, by the British. On the left of this engraving are Washington and Marie-Joseph-Paul-Yves-Roche-Gilbert du Motier, marquis de Lafayette, who brought the army supplies. *(National Archives/DOD, War & Conflict, #36)*

and their captains who were given a letter from either the Continental Congress or, as in the case of many Maryland privateers, from the Patriot government in their state. The letter gave the ship the authority to attack enemy shipping in the name of the Patriot cause. There were more than 1,000 privateers sailing for the American side. Approximately one-quarter of these privateers were from Baltimore and other Maryland ports. Privateers were paid for the captured cargoes, which were often military supplies that were turned over to the Continental army.

MARYLAND LOYALISTS

Not everyone in the colonies was on the Patriot side. It has been estimated that throughout the colonies, one-third of the people considered themselves Patriots, while another third were still neutral at the beginning of the war. The remaining third wanted the colonies to remain part of the British Empire and were called Loyalists. There were a number of Loyalists in Maryland, especially on the Eastern Shore.

Many Maryland Loyalists joined together and fought with the British. Other Loyalists fought against their Patriot neighbors. There are reports of both sides burning crops and homes. The provincial congress passed laws allowing them to take away the property of declared Loyalists. Many Loyalists left Maryland and the other colonies. Some stayed in Maryland, hiding out in the swamps of the Eastern Shore and raiding Patriot homes.

THE END OF THE WAR

In 1778, the British abandoned Philadelphia and turned their attention to the south, first capturing Savannah, Georgia, and then Charleston, South Carolina. From there, the British moved north toward Virginia, which they correctly considered one of the centers of anti-British feelings in the colonies. The British believed that if they could capture Virginia, they would break the Patriot resistance. They might have succeeded had not the French decided to join the Americans in fighting their old enemy.

The addition of French soldiers and the support of the French navy gave Washington the confidence to march south in 1781 to take on the British in his home state. Washington's force consisted

After seven years of fighting, General Cornwallis surrendered at Yorktown on October 17, 1781. *(National Archives)*

of 17,000 American and French soldiers as they surrounded the British led by General Lord Cornwallis at Yorktown, Virginia, in October 1781. Among Washington's soldiers were more than 1,000 "old line" soldiers from Maryland.

With the French navy cutting off any hope of retreat or reinforcements and Washington bombarding their position, Cornwallis took the only path open to him short of losing his entire force. He surrendered on October 19, 1781, and the Americans had won their independence from Great Britain. However, they still faced numerous challenges before the future would look secure.

8

Building a Nation

ARTICLES OF CONFEDERATION

Even before the Second Continental Congress had declared independence, the colonies were faced with a problem. There were no rules that instructed them how a federal government should function. To solve this problem, a committee was formed in June 1776 to propose a set of rules for the national government. John Dickinson of Pennsylvania was selected to chair the committee and is credited as the main writer of the plan that was presented to the congress in 1777. Dickinson's plan called for a relatively strong central government, which immediately ran into problems when it was presented to the congress. Most of the delegates were concerned that a strong central government would simply replace the tyranny of the Crown and Parliament with the tyranny of a federal government.

The delegates at the congress went about amending and rewriting the plan until they came up with what is known as the Articles of Confederation in 1777. This created a central government that was totally at the mercy of the states for operating funds and had very limited power. Under the articles, each individual state government actually had more power than the federal government. Even this watered-down plan for the Articles of Confederation ran into problems, the main one caused by Maryland.

The congress had agreed that the Articles of Confederation would not go into effect until all the states ratified them. Maryland refused to ratify the articles unless some of the larger states, primarily New York and Virginia, gave up their claims to lands west of

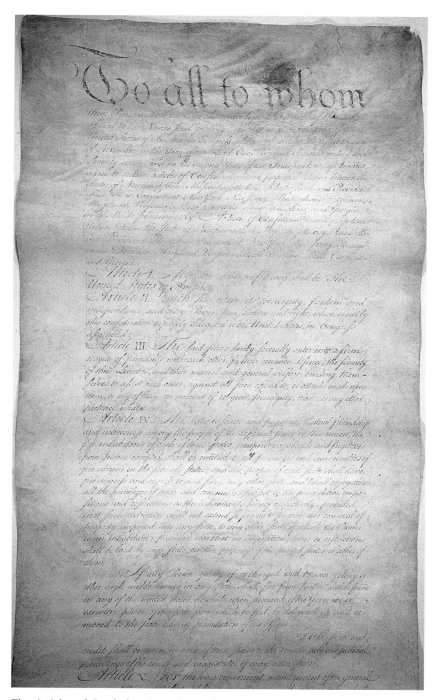

The Articles of Confederation, shown here, were written by a committee of the Continental Congress and intended as a constitution for the colonies.
(National Archives, National Archives Building, NWCTB-360-MISC-ROLL10F81)

the Appalachian Mountains. Maryland and other states feared that if these large states were allowed to expand to the west they would come to dominate the smaller states whose boundaries were already complete. The debate over the western lands went on for almost four years.

Finally, in 1781, New York and Virginia gave up their claims in the west and allowed that land to come under the control of the federal government for future expansion. Maryland had stuck to its guns and won, but with the war over it became almost immediately apparent that the Articles of Confederation were not up to the task of uniting the almost independent 13 states. The federal government could not collect taxes or print money. To pay its bills, the federal government had to go with its hat in its hands and beg the states for funds.

Most of the states gave the federal government only a small portion of what it needed. The situation was so bad that many of the soldiers who had fought in the Revolution had not received all of their pay. In summer 1783, approximately 100 soldiers marched on the hall where the Continental Congress was in session in Philadelphia. These soldiers demanded their back pay. However, the congress had no money. Rather than deal with the soldiers, the congress moved their meetings to Princeton, New Jersey. This brought up a whole new problem.

THE NATIONAL CAPITAL

During the war and the years immediately after, the national capital moved a number of times. Whether they were avoiding the British when they captured Philadelphia or when later they were hiding from angry veterans, the capital had trouble finding a home. It was in Pennsylvania, New Jersey, New York, and Maryland. Baltimore had served as the seat of government from December 20, 1776, to March 4, 1777. Annapolis took its turn as the national capital from November 26, 1783, to June 3, 1784.

New Jersey made a strong bid on more than one occasion for the capital, offering land and money if the government settled there. For many southerners, this was too far north. They wanted the national capital somewhere in the middle. As negotiations took place to try and come up with a national plan to have the federal government take over the states' war debts, Alexander Hamilton

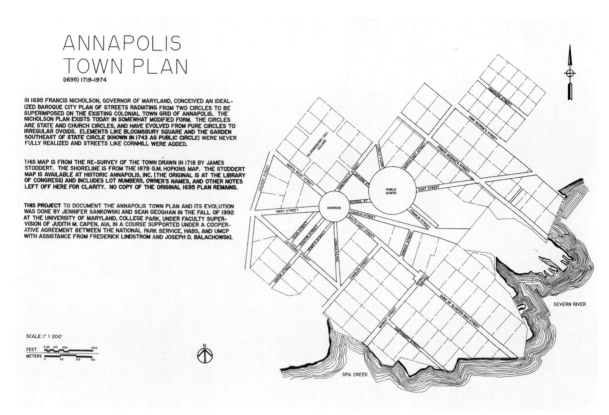

ANNAPOLIS TOWN PLAN
(1695) 1718–1974

IN 1695 FRANCIS NICHOLSON, GOVERNOR OF MARYLAND, CONCEIVED AN IDEAL-IZED BAROQUE CITY PLAN OF STREETS RADIATING FROM TWO CIRCLES TO BE SUPERIMPOSED ON THE EXISTING COLONIAL TOWN GRID OF ANNAPOLIS. THE NICHOLSON PLAN EXISTS TODAY IN SOMEWHAT MODIFIED FORM. THE CIRCLES ARE STATE AND CHURCH CIRCLES, AND HAVE EVOLVED FROM PURE CIRCLES TO IRREGULAR OVOIDS. ELEMENTS LIKE BLOOMSBURY SQUARE AND THE GARDEN SOUTHEAST OF STATE CIRCLE (KNOWN IN 1743 AS PUBLIC CIRCLE) WERE NEVER FULLY REALIZED AND STREETS LIKE CORNHILL WERE ADDED.

THIS MAP IS FROM THE RE-SURVEY OF THE TOWN DRAWN IN 1718 BY JAMES STODDERT. THE SHORELINE IS FROM THE 1878 G.M. HOPKINS MAP. THE STODDERT MAP IS AVAILABLE AT HISTORIC ANNAPOLIS, INC. (THE ORIGINAL IS AT THE LIBRARY OF CONGRESS) AND INCLUDES LOT NUMBERS, OWNER'S NAMES, AND OTHER NOTES LEFT OFF HERE FOR CLARITY. NO COPY OF THE ORIGINAL 1695 PLAN REMAINS.

THIS PROJECT TO DOCUMENT THE ANNAPOLIS TOWN PLAN AND ITS EVOLUTION WAS DONE BY JENNIFER SANKOWSKI AND SEAN GEOGHAN IN THE FALL OF 1992 AT THE UNIVERSITY OF MARYLAND, COLLEGE PARK, UNDER FACULTY SUPER-VISION OF JUDITH M. CAPEN, AIA, IN A COURSE SUPPORTED UNDER A COOPER-ATIVE AGREEMENT BETWEEN THE NATIONAL PARK SERVICE, HABS, AND UMCP WITH ASSISTANCE FROM FREDERICK LINDSTROM AND JOSEPH D. BALACHOWSKI.

SCALE: 1" = 200'

Originally named Anne Arundel Town, Annapolis has been the capital of Maryland since 1694. These plans for the town were drawn in 1718 and based on Governor Francis Nicholson's 1695 plan for the town. Annapolis served as the nation's capital for about seven months from November 1783 to June 1784.
(Library of Congress, Prints and Photographs Division [HABS, MD,2-ANNA,67-1])

made a bargain with Thomas Jefferson. If Jefferson would support Hamilton's financial plans, Hamilton would make sure the national capital was located to the south, and a site in Maryland was chosen to become the national capital—Washington, District of Columbia.

THE NEW CONSTITUTION

Under the Articles of Confederation, more and more problems came to the surface. Each state was free to pursue its own trade policies, and many states functioned like independent countries. In 1785, representatives from Virginia and Maryland met at a conference at Mount Vernon, Virginia. At this meeting, they agreed on a

Washington, District of Columbia

The national capital that was agreed upon by Jefferson and Hamilton was to be something new in the world. It was the first city ever started from scratch to serve as a national capital. Pierre L'Enfant, a French architect and engineer who had served in the Corps of Engineers of the Continental army, was selected to design the new capital. The city was designed to impress visitors with the power of the new United States. However, it grew slowly and did not become a large city until the beginning of the 20th century. During the early part of the 20th century, many impressive buildings were added to the capital, and Washington, District of Columbia, now stands as a testament to the United States that L'Enfant and others had envisioned.

Located on the grounds of the Maryland state house, the old treasury building is the oldest public building in Annapolis. Built in the 1730s, it was first used to issue paper money. *(Library of Congress, Prints and Photographs Division [HABS, MD,2-ANNA,37-2])*

number of solutions to problems that had come up in trade along Chesapeake Bay.

The settlement of these problems led Virginia to suggest that all the states get together and meet in Annapolis, Maryland, in 1786 to discuss other problems relating to commerce. People in some of the states thought this was the job of the congress, while those in other states were just interested in going their own way. In the end, only five states sent delegates to what is known as the Annapolis Convention. The states with representatives at Annapolis were Delaware, New Jersey, New York, Pennsylvania, and Virginia. It was immediately obvious to the delegates that they would not be able to accomplish anything as the Articles of Confederation required that all the states agree to any new laws or rules.

As the delegates discussed the shortcomings of the articles, Alexander Hamilton, one of the New York delegates, suggested that the 13 states should all come together to discuss changes to the articles. Although the Annapolis Convention had no authority to call for a convention, the idea was endorsed by the congress and all the states except Rhode Island sent delegates to Philadelphia in May 1787 to consider changes to the Articles of Confederation.

When the group convened in Philadelphia, the 55 delegates elected George Washington to head what became the Constitutional Convention. The convention really had no authority to do anything beyond working within the Articles of Confederation, making amendments or changes. It was decided to start with a blank page and design a new federal government. Creating a constitution all the delegations could agree on would probably have been impossible, so new rules were created. The language of the new constitution would be subject to a simple majority of the delegates present, and in the end it would go into effect when just nine states had ratified it.

There were many issues that were argued over in front of the whole convention and in the various committees that were instructed to work on the new plan. One of the biggest stumbling blocks was how the states would be represented in the national legislature. There were two opposing plans. The Virginia Plan favored the more populous states by basing representation on population. The small states led by the New Jersey delegation wanted each state to be represented equally. Eventually, they came to what

The Constitutional Convention convened in Philadelphia in May 1787 and remained in session until mid-September. *(Library of Congress, Prints and Photographs Division [LC-USZ62-92869])*

is known as the Great Compromise. The members of the House of Representatives would be apportioned based on the states' populations. The other house, known as the Senate, would have two senators from each state no matter the state's population. This system has worked well for more than 200 years.

Preamble to the U.S. Constitution

We the People of the United States, in Order to form a more perfect Union, establish Justice, insure domestic Tranquility, provide for the common defence, promote the general Welfare, and secure the Blessings of Liberty to ourselves and our Posterity, do ordain and establish this Constitution for the United States of America.

RATIFICATION OF THE CONSTITUTION

Once the new constitution had been passed and signed by the delegates in Philadelphia, it was ready to go to the states for ratification. Maryland had sent five delegates to the Constitutional Convention. They were Daniel Carroll, Luther Martin, James McHenry, John F. Mercer, and Daniel of St. Thomas Jenifer. When it came time for the delegates to sign, Martin and Mercer were upset by the powers granted to the new federal government and refused to sign. The other three delegates' names appear on the constitution.

Maryland played a vital role in the colonies' successful separation from England. The Charles Carroll house in Annapolis, constructed in the late 17th century, is one of the only Declaration of Independence signers' houses still standing. *(Library of Congress, Prints and Photographs Division [HABS, MD,2-ANNA,24-3])*

Delaware became the first state to ratify the new constitution on December 7, 1787. Other states soon followed. In Maryland, a state convention was held in Annapolis in April 1788. On April 28, 1788, Maryland became the seventh state to ratify the constitution, but it did not go into effect until New Hampshire became the ninth state to ratify on June 21, 1788.

Under the new constitution, Maryland took its place as one of the 13 states of the United States and the home of the new national capital. During this time, the economy of Maryland had changed as well. Much of the tobacco land had been used up, and many people in the state turned to the growing industrialization around Baltimore as a source of jobs and wealth. Under the new constitution, the religious freedom that Maryland had been founded on and that had often been a point of conflict in the colony became the law of the land. As the Old Line State, Maryland contributed to the birth of the United States and continues to contribute to the well-being of the country.

Maryland
Time Line

1497

★ John Cabot explores the Eastern Shore of Maryland.

1525

★ Giovanni da Verrazano explores Chesapeake Bay.

1608

★ Captain John Smith explores Chesapeake Bay.

1630

★ William Claiborne establishes a trading post and farming settlement on Kent Island.

1632

★ Cecilius Calvert, second baron Baltimore is granted a charter by Charles I.

1634

★ The *Ark* and *Dove* arrive in Maryland.

1635

★ Claiborne's ship the *Cockatrice* fights the colony's ships.

1645

★ Claiborne seizes power, driving out Governor Leonard Calvert, who flees to Virginia.

1646

★ Calvert regains control of the colony.

1649

★ William Stone, a Protestant, is appointed governor of the colony to appease Parliament during the Civil War in England.
★ Act Concerning Religion is passed by the General Assembly.

1655

★ The Battle of the Severn is fought; Governor William Stone's 130 soldiers are defeated by the Puritans.

1689

★ James II, a Catholic, is succeeded by William and Mary, who are Protestants.

1691

★ William and Mary establish Maryland as a royal colony, with Sir Lionel Copley as governor.

1694

★ Saint Mary's City is replaced as the capital by Anne Arundel Town, which is renamed Annapolis.

1715

★ Maryland becomes a proprietary colony again and is given to Benedict Leonard Calvert, the fourth baron Baltimore.

1729

★ Baltimore is established by charter.

1731

★ The Baltimore Iron Works is started on the Patapsco River.

1755

★ General Edward Braddock goes through Maryland to the west, where his forces are defeated by the French and Indians near Fort Duquesne.

1765

★ Marylander Daniel Dulany's *Considerations on the Propriety of Imposing Taxes in the British Colonies,* which is critical of the Stamp Act, is published in Annapolis.

1774

★ **October 19:** The ship *Peggy Stewart,* with its 2,000 pounds of tax-paid tea, is burned in Annapolis harbor.
★ The First Continental Congress meets in Philadelphia, with Samuel Chase, Robert Goldsborough, Thomas Johnson, William Paca, and Matthew Tilgham representing Maryland.

1776

★ **July 4:** The Declaration of Independence is signed by Maryland representatives William Paca, Charles Carroll, Thomas Stone, and Samuel Chase.

1783

★ **November 26–June 3, 1784:** Annapolis is the national capital.

1786

★ The Annapolis Convention is convened to discuss changes to the Articles of Confederation.

1787

★ The U.S. Constitution is signed by Marylanders Daniel Carroll, James McHenry, and Daniel of St. Thomas Jenifer.

1788

★ **April 28:** Maryland is the seventh state to ratify the U.S. Constitution.

Maryland Historical Sites

ANNAPOLIS

Hammond-Harwood House   Matthew Hammond, a tobacco planter, had this house built starting in 1774.

> *Address:* 19 Maryland Avenue, Annapolis, MD 21401
> *Phone:* 410-263-4683
> *Web Site:* www.hammondharwoodhouse.org

Old Treasury Building   The Old Treasury was built between 1735 and 1737, making it the oldest public building in Maryland. It was built by Patrick Creagh to house the Commissioners for Emitting Bills of Credit.

> *Address:* State Circle, Annapolis, MD 21401
> *Phone:* 800-603-4020
> *Web Site:* www.annapolis.org/treasury2.html

Shiplap House   Built ca. 1715, Shiplap House is one of the oldest houses in Annapolis. It was first lived in by Edward Smith, who operated it as a tavern.

> *Address:* 18 Pinkney Street, Annapolis, MD 21401
> *Phone:* 800-603-4020
> *Web Site:* www.annapolis.org/shiplap2.html

Waterfront Warehouse   The Waterfront Warehouse is a rare example of the tobacco warehouses on the waterfront in the 18th century.

Address: 4 Pinkney Street, Annapolis, MD 21401
Phone: 800-603-4020
Web Site: www.annapolis.org

William Paca House   The William Paca House was built for William Paca between 1763 and 1765. Paca later was one of the signers of the Declaration of Independence and served three terms as governor.

Address: 186 Prince George Street, Annapolis, MD 21401
Phone: 410-267-7619
Web Site: www.annapolis.org/paca2.html

BIG POOL

Fort Frederick State Park   Fort Frederick was begun in 1756, at the beginning of the French and Indian War, by Governor Horatio Sharpe.

Address: 11100 Fort Frederick Road, Big Pool, MD 21711
Phone: 301-842-2155
Web Site: www.dnr.state.md.us/publiclands/ftfrederickhistory.
   html

KINGSVILLE

Jerusalem Mill at Gunpowder Falls State Park   The mill was started in 1769 and started producing flour in 1772. The village also has numerous buildings, including a gun factory, blacksmith shop, and general store.

Address: 2813 Jerusalem Road, Kingsville, MD 21087
Phone: 410-592-2897
Web Site: www.dnr.state.md.us/publiclands/jerusalemhistory.
   html

La Plata

African-American Heritage Society   The African-American Heritage Society shows the life of African Americans in southern Maryland from 1658 to the present.

> *Address:* 7486 Crain Highway, La Plata, MD 20646
> *Phone:* 301-843-0371
> *Web Site:* www.explorecharlescomd.com/sites.htm

Marbury

Smallwood State Park   The Smallwood Retreat House was built ca. 1760 for General William Smallwood.

> *Address:* Box 216, Marbury, MD 20658
> *Phone:* 301-743-7613
> *Web Site:* www.dnr.state.md.us/publiclands/smallwoodhistory.
> html

Port Tobacco

Thomas Stone National Historic Site   Thomas Stone was one of the signers of the Declaration of Independence. His place, Haberdeventure, was built in the early 1770s.

> *Address:* 6655 Rose Hill Road, Port Tobacco, MD 20677
> *Phone:* 301-392-1776
> *Web Site:* www.nps.gov/thst

St. Mary's City

Historic St. Mary's City   Historic St. Mary's City is an 800-acre outdoor museum that portrays life in St. Mary's during its years as the capital of the colony, with a 17th-century plantation, reconstructed state house, and a replica of the square-rigged ship the *Maryland Dove.*

Address: Route 5, St. Mary's City, MD 20686
Phone: 800-762-1634
Web Site: www.stmaryscity.org

TOWSON

Hampton Construction of Hampton was begun in 1783 for Captain Charles Ridgely. On its completion, it was the largest house in the United States.

Address: 535 Hampton Lane, Towson, MD 21286
Phone: 410-823-1309
Web Site: www.nps.gov/hamp

UPPER MARLBORO

Darnall's Chance Built between 1741 and 1742 for James Wardrop, the brick house and its outbuildings are open to the public.

Address: 14800 Governor Oden Bowie Drive, Upper Marlboro, MD 20772
Phone: 301-952-1773
Web Site: www.pgparks.com/places/eleganthistoric/darnalls_history.html

WALDORF

American Indian Cultural Center/Piscataway Indian Museum This museum portrays the life and culture of Native Americans before the coming of the Europeans.

Address: 16812 Country Lane, Waldorf, MD 20601
Phone: 301-372-1932
Web Site: www.explorecharlescomd.com/sites.htm

Further Reading

BOOKS

Britton, Tamara L. *The Maryland Colony.* Edina, Minn.: ABDO, 2001.

Coleman, Brooke. *The Colony of Maryland.* New York: PowerKids, 2000.

Fradin, Dennis Brindell. *The Maryland Colony.* Chicago: Children's Press, 1990.

Land, Aubrey C. *Colonial Maryland: A History.* Millwood, N.Y.: KTO Press, 1981.

Streissguth, Thomas. *Maryland.* San Diego, Calif.: Lucent Books, 2002.

Williams, Jean Kinney. *The Maryland Colony.* Chanhassen, Minn.: Child's World, 2004.

WEB SITES

Maryland. "Kids Room: Early People in Maryland History," Available online. URL: http://www.mdisfun.org/kids/history.asp. Downloaded on November 13, 2004.

Maryland. "Kids Room: Maryland History Timeline," Available online. URL: http://www.mdisfun.org/kids/histime.asp. Downloaded on November 13, 2004.

Maryland. "Maryland Trip Ideas: Tracing the National Road," Available online. URL: http://www.mdisfun.org/destinations/it-nationalrd.asp. Downloaded on November 13, 2004.

Maryland Public Television. "Exploring Maryland's Roots," Available online. URL: http://mdroots.thinkport.org. Downloaded on November 14, 2004.

Maryland State Archives. Available online. URL: http://www.mdarchives.state.md.us. Downloaded on November 13, 2004.

Index

Page numbers in *italic* indicate photographs. Page numbers in **boldface** indicate box features. Page numbers followed by m indicate maps. Page numbers followed by c indicate time line entries. Page numbers followed by t indicate a table or graph.